THE TRANSITION PLAYBOOK

FOR

ATHLETES

HOW ELITE ATHLETES WIN AFTER SPORTS

PHIL COSTA

ROB CURLEY

**EDITED BY
CAROLYN DISBROW**

The Transition Playbook for ATHLETES
How Elite Athletes WIN After Sports
By Phil Costa and Rob Curley
Edited by Carolyn Disbrow

ISBN 978-0-5784-5769-7 (paperback)
ISBN 978-0-5785-0087-4 (hardcover)
ISBN 978-0-57846258-5 (ebook)

An important note: This book is not intended as a substitute for the medical recommendation of physicians or other health-care providers. Rather, it is intended to offer information to help the reader cooperate with physicia.. ˙d health professionals in a mutual quest for optimum well-being.

Book design by Jasmine Oo
Cover design by Clyde Fernando
Illustrated by Milan Colovic, Caricature Empire

First Edition 2019

www.thetransitionplaybook.com

IF NOT YOU,

WHO?

IF NOT NOW,

WHEN?

CONTENTS

THIS BOOK IS PRESENTED WITH ONE GOAL — TO SERVE ATHLETES.

Every year, thousands of athletes transition out of sports into other roles and careers. The majority of these athletes struggle with the adjustment. Our own journey through depression, the loss of identity, and self-doubt was no different.

When we searched for resources to help navigate the transition, we found two types of books: those written by academics, and those written by former athletes. The academics wrote **as if** they never played sports, using language better suited for a university classroom. The athletes wrote **only** about their experience, surrounding great advice with 200 pages of biography.

We felt there had to be a better way to impact today's athletes. So, we reached out to experts and former college, professional, and Olympic athletes to support the next generation.

This book features more than 100 athletes from over 30 different sports. They highlight areas where transitioning athletes need guidance. Their advice is short and to the point.

These athletes speak from firsthand experiences. Some are world famous. Others are known to no one outside their immediate family. We draw no distinction. The transition connects us all. Here is the best advice for finding success after sports.

This is the book we were searching for.

A FEW THINGS TO CONSIDER WHILE READING:

1. Take out something to write with; mark-up, bend the pages, or highlight areas you find inspiring. Then revisit your notes when you need encouragement.

2. In some cases, athletes share their experiences and feelings, but offer no actionable advice. We found this important to include because relating with someone else's situation can help you better identify and handle your own. Shared experiences are powerful teachers.

3. The athletes in this book offer some contradictory advice. Just like in sports, there are many ways to win. Some teams win because of their defense, while others win with offense. All roads lead to victory.

4. You will love some of the advice shared here. Some may not relate to your situation at all. These are tools, not rules. Learn from these athletes' experiences. Take what you need and leave the rest.

THE QUESTIONS

ROUTINE

What advice would you give as the first step to creating a successful routine after sports? What are the essentials in your own routine?

FAILURE

How has a failure helped pave the way for future success?

GUIDANCE

What advice do you have for recent student-athlete graduates about searching for and discovering a new passion?

LESSON

What was the greatest lesson learned from sports that prepared you for post-sport professional success?

INSPIRATION

What encouragement or advice do you have for athletes currently struggling with the transition?

GROWTH

Scroll through your phone, which apps would your 'former athlete-self' be surprised to see?

CHALLENGE

What was your biggest challenge and how did you overcome it?

PREPARATION

What preparations did you make for life after sports while you were still an athlete? What you would have done differently?

RESOURCES

Which resources would be helpful for athletes going through this transitional period?

MENTOR

What are helpful tips for finding a mentor? What are the traits of a great mentee?

EXPERT TO NOVICE

When you were a novice in your new field, what were your greatest obstacles?

The content has been edited and condensed from its original format for clarity. Please find additional questions in the back of the book.

THE TRANSITION PLAYBOOK

FOR

ATHLETES

HOW ELITE ATHLETES WIN AFTER SPORTS

DANNY OQUENDO

IG: @TheKingOquendo | Twitter: @TheKingOquendo | LinkedIn: Daniel Oquendo

A dual-sport athlete in track and football at the University of Maryland. Danny was awarded the 2016 McGuire Family Advocacy Award for his dedication to serving young people with disabilities. He was named 2017 "Law Student of the Year" by National Jurist. In 2018, he graduated Magna Cum Laude from New York Law School. Today, Danny works as a Lawyer for one of the top firms in NYC and is a special education advocate.

GUIDANCE

Don't feel pressured to transition into something immediately, you will only stress yourself out. Research different fields and professions. Hell, it took me 6 years after my last game to find the motivation to go to law school. Take your time and don't compare your path to anyone else's.

INSPIRATION

This one is more for college athletes who didn't make it professionally. Do not be ashamed. In fact, feel pride and gratitude. You have made it further than most. You have the rest of your life ahead of you, not behind you.

Any time spent dwelling on what could have been is time better spent honing new crafts for your transition towards a new and fulfilling life.

GROWTH

Acorn: an app to invest spare change from credit and debit card purchases.

Wall Street Journal: my transition out of athlete life and into adulthood included the realization that I had to be in tune with the world outside of my echo chamber.

"TO BE GREAT, IS TO BE MISUNDERSTOOD."
RALPH WALDO EMERSON

PREPARATION

During college I taught myself guitar, I learned how to write code, and I took creative writing workshops. Being well-rounded is invaluable to many employers. The more non-sports specific things you can be involved in while an athlete, the better your life will be after sports.

ROUTINE

Transitioning from a strict routine was tough. I recommend getting in the habit of using a calendar. Much like having a coach, it forces me to stay true to my responsibilities. I start and end my days with a glance at my calendar to prepare and get my mind right for the day ahead.

RESOURCES

In Tune with the Infinite by Ralph Waldo Trine.

When my athletic career ended, I dove head first into a state of depression. I was working a low paying job, with no sign of a fulfilling career in sight. This book practically saved my life.

SUMMER SANDERS

IG: @summersanders_ | FB: Summer Sanders | summersanders.co

Back-to-back NCAA Swimmer of the Year, and eight-time NCAA National Champion. Summer is a two-time Olympic gold medalist. She won four medals at the '92 Olympic Games in Barcelona, setting an Olympic record in the 200-meter butterfly. While competing, Summer began her career in TV and broadcasting. She has appeared on NBA Inside Stuff, Good Morning America, and Inside Out with Summer Sanders. Today, Summer continues her work as a Sports Commentator and TV Host.

ROUTINE

I like to exercise first thing in the morning so I don't spend all day thinking about when I'm going to fit in my workout. Start your day with some simple accomplishments so that you are ready to focus on what's next.

FAILURE

Don't be afraid to fail in the next phase of life. The best way to figure out what you really want to do is by ruling out the things you really don't want to do.

It's interesting how many athletes making the transition expect instant gratification. It's as if they forgot how hard they had to work to get to where they got in their sport. Maybe they feel the work they put into their sport should give them extra points in their next phase. It doesn't work that way.

Remember how you became an elite athlete — hard work, dedication, determination, self-discipline and learning from failure.

PREPARATION

When you are at the top of your sport, you meet so many people who could help influence your next career. You should ask for their information and follow-up. Allow these people to be a part of your process, and show them that you are interested in working hard beyond your sport.

TREY MONTGOMERY

IG: @CoachT_Meaux | Twitter: @CoachT_Meaux | FB: Trey Pearson Montgomery

A two-year captain for the Samford University Men's Basketball Team. Trey was a two-time recipient of the program's Kevy McInnis Award, given to the player who best demonstrates leadership both on and off the court. He continued his career professionally in the NBA Developmental League for the Albuquerque Thunderbirds. He played two seasons in Germany for the Giessen Pointers, and two seasons in the ABA for the Jackson Showboats. Today, Trey serves as an Assistant Coach for the University of Pennsylvania Men's Basketball Team.

GROWTH

As I've gotten older, I've come to understand the importance of being informed. I now read and listen to Apple Books, TED Talks, and CNN.

ROUTINE

I like to have a plan for the day, rather than a routine. I make a checklist of what I want to accomplish and how I want to complete it. This helps me prioritize.

INSPIRATION

It's never as good or as bad as it seems. It's always what you make of it.

MENTOR

My dad would always tell me, "It's okay to be a copycat, as long as you copy the right cat."

Most people fail with mentors because they just seek out the most successful person they know.

That's terrible advice.

My mentor started off as a peer. Find someone who can be honest and transparent with you.

CHALLENGE

I was always known as the basketball player. I had to learn who I was without basketball; it took a while. By putting myself in different settings, I learned about myself. Ask yourself:

Do I prefer spending time at the bookstore or the theater?

If I have $100, what do I do with it?

Those small things add up to who you are as a person outside of sports.

PAM DURKIN

IG: @Coach_P_Durk | Twitter: @CoachPDurk | FB: Pam Durkin | LinkedIn: Pamela A Durkin

College Basketball

Associate Head Coach Women's Basketball, Rider University

MENTOR

Don't be afraid to ask. And don't assume that person is too busy for you. A great mentor is someone who asks difficult questions, and makes you think outside the box.

CHALLENGE

In a sport full of scholarships, teaching players about money is critically important. My players don't need to work to pay for their college education. Once they graduate and start making money, it's easy to want to spend it right away. The power of financial literacy cannot be overstated.

RESOURCES

Podcast:

Sets For Life by Joi Walker.

Books:

Chop Wood, Carry Water by Joshua Medcalf.

Drive by Daniel Pink.

BOB FITZPATRICK

IG: @fitzparc | Twitter: @fitzparc | LinkedIn: Bob FitzPatrick

College Lacrosse
Medical Device Sales

MENTOR

No one knows everything. Don't have just one mentor – learn as much as you can from as many people as you can. Take their best qualities and create your own strategy.

"CONFIDENCE IS THE KEY TO ALL THE LOCKS."

KEVIN MINIEFIELD

IG: @kevinminiefield | Twitter: @Kmini3 | FB: Kevin Miniefield | LinkedIn: Kevin Miniefield

Professional Football
Coordinator of Former Student-Athlete Development, Arizona State University

GUIDANCE

I've learned that whatever you do well with the least amount of effort is considered your gift. I've also learned that sometimes your gift doesn't align with your passion. This is an opportunity to reinvent yourself. Search for what excites and scares you at the same time.

ADAM KREEK

IG: @adamkreek | Twitter: @adamkreek | FB: Adam Kreek | LinkedIn: Adam Kreek | kreekspeak.com

An Olympic rower representing Canada, Adam won gold at the 2008 Summer Olympics in the Men's Eight competition. He also won gold at the 2002, 2003, and 2007 World Championships. In 2013, Adam and three teammates attempted to row from Africa to North America. Their journey ended after 73 days when their boat capsized in the Bermuda Triangle. He discusses this courageous journey in his TEDx Talk: *I Seek Failure*. Today, Adam works as a Management Consultant and Executive Coach.

EXPERT TO NOVICE

Get ready to be horrible at something new. The trick is to find something you can enjoy being horrible at. That's the path to next excellence. Then, embrace the grind.

INSPIRATION

Humility teaches you what really matters in life and helps you see the lies of youthful success.

"WHEN TWO OR THREE AGREE ON A COMMON PURPOSE, THEN NOTHING IS IMPOSSIBLE."

JIM ROHN

ROUTINE

My routine includes time with my children and my wife. I also spend time with other men who share my ambition, drive, and need for physical challenge.

RESOURCES

The War of Art by Steven Pressfield: defines the inner demons you must tame to create something of lasting significance.

Going to Pieces Without Falling Apart by Mark Epstein: concepts on how to move forward when feeling broken.

CHALLENGE

My biggest challenge was finding the right focus. I had a driving ambition and it felt like I could do anything in the world. I just didn't know where to focus my energy.

FAILURE

One of the first times I delivered a motivational speech, my tongue and throat froze up. Nothing. Came. Out. The audience felt horrible for me. Learning that I could fail in front of others and still be OK was remarkably empowering.

I also learned that success is not necessarily transferable. Just because you were good at sports doesn't mean that you will be a good communicator. You still have to work your butt off to be good at the next thing. The work never ends.

YEMI OYEFUWA

IG: @topnerdsuperpoet | Twitter: @yemSTAR14 | FB: Yemi Oyefuwa | sixfootsomething.wordpress.com

College & Semi-Professional Basketball

TV Casting, Producer and Writer

ROUTINE

Create your own routine outside of and unrelated to your sport. I always had hobbies outside of basketball that I could potentially turn into a career. I indulged in those hobbies as frequently as my schedule allowed. This helped me build a foundation of confidence outside of sports.

MENTOR

Be honest about your goals with your mentor so they can be honest whether or not they can help.

> "LIFE IMITATES ART FAR MORE THAN
> ART IMITATES LIFE."
> OSCAR WILDE

CHRIS GRONKOWSKI

IG: @chrisgronkowski | Twitter: @chrisgronkowski | FB: Ice Shaker Bottle | LinkedIn: Chris Gronkowski | iceshaker.com & everythingdecorated.com

An NFL player for the Dallas Cowboys, Denver Broncos, and Indian-apolis Colts. After football, Chris co-founded Everything Decorated, a successful online custom engraving company. In 2017, his next venture, Ice Shaker, was featured on Shark Tank where he secured investment from both Mark Cuban and Alex Rodriguez. Today, Chris owns and operates two multi-million dollar businesses.

ROUTINE

Routine has been crucial for my success. I start my day with a workout or something that gets me up and moving. It could be playing a game of pick-up basketball or moving boxes in the warehouse. This is a great way for me to release stress and plan my day. I attack the most important projects while I am fresh and alert.

EXPERT TO NOVICE

My greatest obstacle was exposure. I had no idea how to market my prod-ucts or educate consumers.

No matter how great your products are, if no one knows about them, they will never sell. I wasn't shy about reaching out to other entrepreneurs to find these answers.

LESSON

Being an entrepreneur is very much like being an athlete. Your failure or success depends on you. I like to have proof of concept before I dive all-in on a business. Once I can say that customers definitely want the product, then all the doubt is gone, and it is time to go to work.

Business is tough and you will end up doing a ton of tasks that you never thought you would be doing. Just like a sports career, there are ups and downs, but the harder you work the more successful you will be. Paychecks do not come easy at first. By continuing to put in the hard work and long days, the big paychecks will come.

"SUCCESS ISN'T ALWAYS ABOUT 'GREATNESS', IT'S ABOUT CONSISTENCY. CONSISTENT, HARD WORK GAINS SUCCESS. GREATNESS WILL COME."
DWAYNE "THE ROCK" JOHNSON

JORDAN ELKINS

IG: @jordanelkins_ & @innergy__ | FB: Jordan Elkins | LinkedIn: Jordan Elkins | innergyalaska.com

College Ice Hockey

Owner, Innergy Fitness Studio

INSPIRATION

Your dream job might not even exist yet.

"GO CONFIDENTLY IN THE DIRECTION OF YOUR DREAMS, LIVE THE LIFE YOU'VE IMAGINED."

HENRY DAVID THOREAU

PREPARATION

You never know when opportunities will arise.

Senior year, I was on an airplane when I noticed some young female hockey players and struck up a conversation. I invited them to tour our college facility, watch practice, and meet my teammates. The next day our locker room was full of teenage hockey players and their parents. I had no idea the President of the Dallas Stars Youth Organization was among them. This led to a job offer with the organization after college.

If I hadn't been proud of my school, my team, and who I was in that moment, I would have never reached out to those people or extended an offer for them to visit.

Enjoy where you are, even if you don't exactly know where you are going. Do the best with what you have and everything will turn out fine.

JULIA MANCUSO

IG: @juliamancuso | Twitter: @juliamancuso | FB: Julia Mancuso
USA | juliamancuso.com

A four-time Olympic medalist, Julia won Giant Slalom gold at the 2006 Winter Olympics Games in Turin. Known as "Super Jules," she is a leading advocate for the advancement of women's sports. Julia is a Philanthropist, Entrepreneur, and Brand Ambassador for companies such as GoPro, Spyder, and Stöckli.

LESSON

Discipline and accountability for sure. Show up and do what you say you will.

INSPIRATION

Find your passion. What inspires YOU? What is YOUR goal in life? That's it. I think society puts expectations on everyone, but it really comes down to living YOUR best life.

CHALLENGE

Sports have an amazing way of bringing everyone together. When it's over, it can feel both abrupt and lonely. I find that social media has helped me a lot with networking.

> "BELIEVE YOU CAN OR BELIEVE YOU CAN'T.
> EITHER WAY YOU ARE RIGHT."
> *HENRY FORD*

PREPARATION

I think the number one thing is financial preparation. I come from a family of entrepreneurs so I learned at a young age about saving. You have to save for the future right now.

RESOURCES

You Are a Badass by Jen Sincero.

I love listening to *The Tim Ferriss Show* podcast. I find him so interesting and inspiring.

EXPERT TO NOVICE

I realize how much I improve as I put more hours into things. It's not all natural skill and ability :) Put in your hours!

TYWANNA SMITH

IG: @TywannaDSmith | Twitter: @TywannaDSmith | FB: Tywanna Smith | LinkedIn: Tywanna Smith

Captain and four-year starter for the University of Mississippi Women's Basketball Team. After graduating, Tywanna continued her career professionally in Spain and the Netherlands, where she was named a Dutch FEB All-Star. Tywanna returned home to launch The Athlete's Nexus, a sports marketing and business management company. The company's mission is to advise athletes regarding finances, branding, and business.

ROUTINE

Take the time to prepare. Athletes are used to making split-second decisions in game situations. By slowing down, we force ourselves to think and consider alternatives. This helps us make better decisions.

"THE PRICE OF GREATNESS IS RESPONSIBILITY."
WINSTON CHURCHILL

PREPARATION

I networked like crazy! I connected with all types of people, treated them kindly, and made sure to reach out to them a few times a year just to say 'HI.'

LESSON

I learned everything will not always go my way. There are obstacles outside of my control. And even when I do everything right, things can still go wrong. I learned the only person I can control is myself. I began focusing on the things I'm responsible for – my attitude, my effort, and my activity.

RESOURCES

Relentless: From Good to Great to Unstoppable by Tim Grover. Tim trained Michael Jordan, Kobe Bryant, and Dwyane Wade. In his book, he details different levels of mental focus and how they can determine your level of success. I re-read it a few times a year.

JON HARRIS

IG: @athlifer | Twitter: @jharrisathlife | FB: Jon Harris | LinkedIn: Jon Harris | athlifefoundation.org

A college basketball player, Jon was a four-year letterman at DePaul University. He is the Founder and CEO of AthLife Enterprises — servicing the education, career development, and life skill needs of athletes. AthLife works with the NFL Players Association, the Trust (powered by the NFLPA), NBA, National Basketball Retired Players Association, the NBA Players Legacy Fund, MLS, MLS Players Union, WWE, with student-athletes at more than 40 colleges and more than 10,000 high school student-athletes across the US. Jon has found success post-sport by combining two of his passions, sports and philanthropy.

ROUTINE

The less athletes prepare for that inevitable day, the harder it will be to transition effectively to that next thing. I challenge athletes to account for how they fill their free time in-season, how they spend off-days, and unstructured parts of the off-season.

100% of athletes will do something other than play competitive sports at some point in their life.

"THE BEST WAY TO PREDICT THE FUTURE
IS TO CREATE IT."

ABRAHAM LINCOLN

INSPIRATION

You will struggle to some degree with the transition from a life dedicated to sport. It's OK to feel loss, and a positive way to overcome this feeling is to work towards the next goal.

MENTOR

Develop a pipeline. Start cultivating relationships today. *LinkedIn* is a key tool for this. You can see what people are doing, what they're interested in, and their professional network.

Begin by having short meetings to develop rapport with potential mentors. It takes TIME to develop these relationships. Do not ask to be mentored in the first meeting.

Remember to be considerate of your mentor's time. If they are worth it, they will be busy. I ask for 5-15 minutes and make sure to stick to that amount of time.

GUIDANCE

Pursue your interests. If you wait around for the perfect experience, you'll never have anything to show on your resume.

See all those fancy people standing on the sidelines at games or practice? Get their business cards and connect with them. They want to help you if they can. When you become a former player, they often become less interested in helping if they didn't know you when you were a player.

RESOURCES

Follow me on *LinkedIn*. I share inspirational stories of athletes who've made remarkable transitions. (linkedin.com/jonharris)

AthLife Fundamentals: a blog on athlete career transition topics. (athlife.com)

RYLER DEHEART

IG: @rdeheart | Twitter: @RylerDeHeart I FB: Ryler DeHeart I LinkedIn: Ryler DeHeart

Professional Tennis

Tennis Coach, Florida State University

INSPIRATION

Take comfort in knowing that almost everyone struggles through their transition. It's normal to feel lost.

It's really not so much about WHAT you do. It's HOW you do it that counts!

RESOURCES

Grit by Angela Duckworth.

Champion Minded by Allistair McCaw.

These phenomenal books illustrate why the development of toughness, character, and mindset are vital ingredients for success.

LESSON

A great coach of mine always said, "Get 1% better today!" There are so many lessons to be learned through sports that can be applied to the real world. Focus on getting just a little bit better every day.

ELI CRANOR

Twitter: @elicranor | elicranor.com

Professional Football

Author

ROUTINE

I like to follow Habit 3: Put First Things First from Stephen Covey's *The 7 Habits of Highly Effective People*. In other words, do the things that matter right off the bat, early in the morning.

Don't stray too far from the discipline you had as an athlete. The reason we had such regimented schedules was to achieve the very tangible goal of winning. The same is true in business and life. You wake up every day and win or lose, there's just not a scoreboard anymore.

"IF YOU CAN FILL THE UNFORGIVING MINUTE WITH SIXTY SECONDS WORTH OF DISTANCE RUN, THEN YOURS IS THE EARTH AND EVERYTHING THAT'S IN IT, AND WHICH IS MORE, YOU'LL BE A MAN, MY SON."

RUDYARD KIPLING

INSPIRATION

Find something that gets you out of bed in the morning and do it with all you have.

RESOURCES

The 7 Habits of Highly Effective People by Stephen Covey.

Good to Great by Jim Collins.

Zen and the Art of Motorcycle Maintenance by Robert Pirsig.

EXPERT TO NOVICE

The hardest thing is not knowing if you're good enough or if your time is ever going to pay off, but none of that matters if you're doing something you love. Besides, there's only one way to figure out if you're good enough, and that's to go out and do it.

DR. C. KEITH HARRISON

A football player at West Texas A&M University. Today, Dr. Harrison is the Associate Chief Academic Officer for the DeVos Sport Business Management Program. His brief list of clients and partnerships include the Miami Dolphins, University of Oregon, Jordan Brand, UCLA, and Penn's Wharton School. Dr. Harrison serves as the Principal Investigator and Lead Researcher for the NFL and NFL Player Engagement research series reports.

INSPIRATION

Learn to ball out in life, work, and family. That means competing in everything that you do. You possess the skills. You just have to shift your mindset.

RESOURCES

My website scholarballer.org is focused on inspiring youth and young adults to develop leadership skills and to excel in education and life.

PREPARATION

Internships, volunteering, and developing an identity outside of your comfort zone will help a great deal.

The transferable skills (persistence, determination, goal-setting, leadership, teamwork) athletes learn from sports are valuable to any organization.

"WHEN IT COMES TO WINNING VERSUS LOSING, THE OUTCOME IS OFTEN BEYOND OUR CONTROL. HOWEVER, WHEN IT COMES TO NEVER GIVING UP VERSUS QUITTING, THE CHOICE IS OURS AND WHAT WE CHOOSE WILL MOST LIKELY BECOME OUR DESTINY."

DR. C. KEITH HARRISON

ANGELIQUE "ANGEL" HALL BOVEE

IG: @angelbovee | Twitter: @angelbovee | FB: motivationalspeakerangelbovee | LinkedIn: Angelique Bovee | boxingangel.com

In 2001, Angel was crowned the US Light Middleweight boxing champion, finishing the year as the #1 ranked female in the USA. In 2002, she moved down two weight classes and won gold, this time as a Light Welterweight. Angel represented Team USA at the first two World Championships ever contested for female boxers. In 2017, she was elected to serve on the IOC's Athlete Career Program Steering Committee. Today, Angel works as a Career Coach for Team USA athletes and as a Motivational Speaker, advocating for and sharing her experiences as an out LGBT athlete.

MENTOR

Look for a compassionate leader who is both honest and empathetic. It's not uncommon to have different mentors for different stages of your journey.

SUPPORT

Few female athletes have the opportunity for long-term financial security. Even those at the pinnacle of their sport often earn very little money. This presents significant challenges when women retire. To change this we need greater female representation in sports leadership, administration, and coaching. This is not an easy task and there have been many institutionalized barriers put in place to prevent women from entering these leadership positions. To succeed, female athletes need to have courage to face these institutions head-on and demand equity. Courage is contagious!

PREPARATION

When I competed for Team USA, female boxers received zero financial support. So I had to be scrappy. I trained full-time and worked a host of part-time jobs to make ends meet. I tried everything from seasonal national park ranger to personal trainer, pool operator, real estate assistant, and videographer.

I taught myself how to create sponsorship proposals, built my own website, and wrote my own press releases to market myself. Through these experiences I actively developed skills outside of the ring that I now rely on in the corporate world.

GUIDANCE

Your status as an athlete gives you access to people that you won't necessarily have access to when you are out of sports. Take advantage of that!

LESSON

People often ask what was the biggest challenge I had to face in boxing.

Was it living in my car to afford to train full-time? Was it being a visible LGBT athlete at a time when that was considered a huge risk? Was it the pressure of a big match or the risk of getting hurt?

While all those things were difficult, the biggest obstacle I encountered was outside the ring, fighting for gender equality in the sport.

This journey has taught me lessons I call the four R's. . . creating a Roadmap, Risk-taking, Resiliency, and Redefinition. Boxing has given me not only a skill set to deal with adversity, but also the confidence to know that I can face whatever life throws my way.

"FIND A WAY."
DIANA NYAD

PHIL COSTA

IG: @costa_phil | Twitter: @PhilCosta67 | FB: Phil Costa | LinkedIn: Phil Costa | thetransitionplaybook.com

Former starting center for the Dallas Cowboys, Phil played in the NFL from 2010-2014. After football, he worked for a medical device company, assisting heart surgeons during more than 500 operations. Phil earned his MBA from Columbia Business School in 2018, and has traveled to more than 25 countries including South Africa, Vietnam, and Japan. Today, he's enrolled in Spanish language school in Madrid and is working on his next book.

INSPIRATION

I struggled too. Reach out to someone to seek encouragement or advice if you're having a hard time during your transition. Connect with me at thetransitionplaybook.com

FAILURE

As a player for the Dallas Cowboys, fans are excited to meet you and will wait in line for your autograph. My next job was a much different experience.

Early in my career as a pacemaker sales representative, I was making a sales call at a doctor's office. As I approached the secretary's desk, the doctor appeared. He looked at me and without saying a word, shook his head "NO" and walked away.

Less than 18 months prior, people were paying a lot of money to spend time with me. Now, I couldn't even get a few minutes of this doctor's time. I got humbled real quick. I realized that things had changed and I had better change with them.

GROWTH

Wall Street Journal: the first time I read the WSJ it was like reading another language and I constantly had to use a dictionary. It gets easier over time.

Fluenz: if you're someone who loves a challenge, try learning another language. It's proven to be one of the most rewarding things I've ever done.

CorePower Yoga: it's my form of meditation while getting a kick-ass workout.

"WIN THE DAY"

GUIDANCE

Be RELENTLESS in your search.

After the NFL, I spent time with experts in fields that interested me. I set up meetings with lawyers, politicians, broadcasters, doctors, coaches, real estate investors and politicians. When you're a professional athlete opportunities come to you, but after sports YOU have to create the opportunities. When they're done playing many athletes say, *the phone stops ringing*. This is true. So, MAKE IT RING by proactively reaching out to people.

RESOURCES

6 Rules for Success by Arnold Schwarzenegger (youtube.com).

How to Win Friends and Influence People by Dale Carnegie.

WIN THE DAY. Put everything you have into today. Then go and do the same thing tomorrow. Success is the sum of thousands of little victories.

My coach for the Dallas Cowboys would say, "There is trying and there is doing. This is the NFL, EVERYONE TRIES. You either get the job done or you don't. And if you don't, I'll find someone who will." I continue to act with that same sense of urgency today.

TAYLOR DOUCET

IG: @Tedi65 | FB: Tedi Doucet | LinkedIn: Taylor Doucet

College Volleyball
Risk Advisory Services, Ernst & Young

ROUTINE

Find your source of energy and prioritize time each week for it. I often travel from Sunday to Thursday for work, but I make sure to schedule one night free to relax and focus on myself.

CHALLENGE

Following my retirement, I struggled with self-confidence. Growing up, I played on successful teams, which gave me an abundance of confidence throughout my career. After my last match, I felt excitement about the future but also uncertainty and doubt. Volleyball was how I distinguished myself from peers, so the uncertainty of my new identity was terrifying for me.

RESOURCES

Lean In: Women, Work, and the Will to Lead by Sheryl Sandberg. I recommend this book to any ambitious female as she tackles the professional world for the first time.

LESSON

My greatest takeaway from sports was being surrounded by people who possess complimentary talents to my own. Today, I find my strongest project teams are composed of colleagues who bring a different skill set than my own.

SCOTT DONIE

IG: @ScottDonie & @ColumbiaDiving | Twitter: @ScottDonie & @ColumbiaDiving | FB: Columbia Diving

Olympic Diving

Head Coach Men's and Women's Diving, Columbia University

PREPARATION

Nothing can prepare you better than your own experiences. I took public speaking classes and worked a variety of jobs to prepare for life after sports.

LESSON

Be humble and ask for help. Approach each day with the mindset of a beginner.

"DO NOT LET WHAT YOU CANNOT DO INTERFERE
WITH WHAT YOU CAN DO."
JOHN WOODEN

BRIAN HUNTER

IG: @bhunter1426 | Twitter: @bhunter1426 | FB: Brian Hunter

Professional Baseball
Baseball Scout

ROUTINE

My advice is to take it slow. Especially in the beginning — develop a routine that is both easy to follow and satisfies you.

GUIDANCE

The most common mistake professional athletes make is not wanting to have a game plan for when they are done playing. Research opportunities while you're still an athlete.

"SOMEONE IS ALWAYS WATCHING."

SHANNON MILLER

IG: @shannonmiller96 | Twitter: @shannonmiller96 | FB: Shannon Miller Official | LinkedIn: Shannonmiller96 | shannonmiller.com

Seven-time Olympic medalist. Her tally of five medals at the '92 Olympics was the most medals won by a US athlete in any sport. At the '96 Games, she led the "Magnificent Seven" to the US Women's first Team Gold and for the first time for any American, she captured gold on Balance Beam. Shannon then earned her marketing and entrepreneurship degrees from the University of Houston and a law degree from Boston College. She now serves as the President of Shannon Miller Enterprises (devoted to women's health), a Gymnastics Analyst, and Professional Speaker.

ROUTINE

The sudden lack of structure after retirement can be jarring. Fill your time with positive activities that hold you accountable to learning and growing. The earlier you establish structure, the easier your transition will be.

INSPIRATION

Medals are not won on the day of competition, they are won with the hard work and preparation that happened years before stepping on the competition floor. It's the work we do each day, even when it's not glamorous, that makes it happen.

"DON'T JUDGE ME BY MY SUCCESSES, BUT RATHER HOW MANY TIMES I FELL AND GOT BACK UP AGAIN."

NELSON MANDELA

PREPARATION

I began taking college classes while training for my last Olympics. Education was my constant, and it was important for me to have at least one thing that didn't change overnight when I retired.

LESSON

No one wants to stumble or fall. But when we do, we learn more than we ever could if we never tried. Understand that failure is part of the path to success.

If you don't fail at some point, you're not challenging yourself enough. When you fail, you learn to get back up. You learn that it may not be easy, but it's worth it!

EXPERT TO NOVICE

When I first launched my company, my business partner and I were the marketing team, accounting department, growth strategy, web designer, the coffee-getter, face of the company and had 100 other responsibilities. As we began to grow, I fell into the trap of thinking I had to do it all.

That changed when I was diagnosed with cancer six months after we launched. I needed to focus on my health so I took a back seat. I let go of some responsibilities and allowed my team to do what they do best. Today, I'm learning a great deal from them and we are growing stronger and faster together.

TIM MORRIS

IG: @timmyraym | Twitter: @coachtimmorris

Professional Basketball

College Basketball Coach

ROUTINE

Take ownership of your schedule. Good athletes follow the schedule that their coaches set for them. Great athletes and high achievers create their own schedule based on their goals. Hold yourself to a higher standard.

PREPARATION

During college, I was a member of the NCAA Student-Athlete Advisory Committees (SAACs). This gave me leadership and teamwork experience in a setting outside of athletics and prepared me to navigate the post-collegiate world. I also interned and shadowed professionals in medicine, banking, and tech.

RESOURCES

Extreme Ownership by Jocko Willink and Leif Babin.

Shoe Dog by Phil Knight.

LESSON

Treat your new profession like a competition. Study the game and master the fundamentals to excel in your role.

JIMMY PEDRO

Twitter: @JimmyPedroUSA | FB: Jimmy Pedro | LinkedIn: Jimmy Pedro | jimmypedro.com & pedrosjudo.com

A two-time Olympic bronze medalist, World Judo Champion, and four-time "Player of the Year." Jimmy was inducted into the Black Belt Hall of Fame in 1997. He coached at the 2012 and 2016 Olympic Games, and led his players to back-to-back gold medals. Jimmy founded Pedro's Judo Center and works as President of FUJI Mats and Vice President of Hatashita.

PREPARATION

When I was competing and pursuing my Olympic dream, I never put my "regular life" on hold. I continued my studies as a college athlete and got my degree from Brown University.

Immediately after college, I got married, had kids, moved to Japan and began training full-time for the Olympics. I believe that being an athlete, student, father, and husband, ultimately led me to be more successful than if I had only been an athlete.

"FAILING TO PREPARE IS PREPARING TO FAIL."
BENJAMIN FRANKLIN

Perseverance is the greatest lesson I learned from sports. To become a champion, I had to learn to how to train smarter, harder, and push through the tough times. Today, I rely on these same principles for professional success.

EXPERT TO NOVICE

My greatest obstacle was taking the risk to go out on my own and start my own company. I left a salaried position with benefits at a large company. I had three children and was unsure if I could make enough money to support my family. But, my wife believed in me and encouraged me to take the chance because I would be doing what I loved.

In life, you have to take risks to reap the rewards. More than a decade later, I own three successful companies in the martial arts field. I work non-stop and love what I do, making 10x the money as before.

DAVIN MEGGETT

IG: @Meggett_Tron | Twitter: @Meggett_Tron | FB:Davin Meggett

Professional Football
Special Education Teacher

INSPIRATION

You were never ONLY an athlete. Don't let the world convince you otherwise.

"IN ORDER TO BE GREAT, YOU MUST GET COMFORTABLE BEING UNCOMFORTABLE."

DAVE PHILISTIN

Professional Football
CEO, Technology Firm

LESSON

D2: Dedication & Discipline. Mastering these skills gives me an advantage because I know what it means to work relentlessly towards success.

"YOU CAN TAKE MY BODY. YOU CAN TAKE
MY BONES. YOU CAN TAKE MY BLOOD.
BUT NOT MY SOUL."
RHIANNON GIDDENS

JOHN DISCHERT

IG: @johndish | FB: John Dischert | LinkedIn: John Dischert

College Baseball
Anti-Money Laundering Investigator

GROWTH

Mint: this helps me manage my finances.

CreditKarma: if I understood the importance of having and maintaining good credit then I would have taken a more proactive approach when I was younger.

LinkedIn: the idea of networking with other business professionals is something I never thought I would need.

CHALLENGE

It was a real gut check moment to look myself in the mirror and tell myself that my playing days were over. I felt like I lost my identity. The fear of taking a step in the wrong direction that would turn into the next ten years of my life was crippling for me.

I made a commitment to refocus all of my motivation and competitiveness in a new direction. In time, I learned that baseball does not define me, rather it instilled in me the discipline, commitment, and values that make me the person I am today.

LESSON

Humility. A key to success in my playing days was never underestimating anyone. Therefore, I never changed my approach based on my opponent. This has served me well.

My father instilled words in me at a young age that I carry with me to this day. "As hard as you think you are working right now, there is someone out there working harder than you."

OBUMNEME AKUNYILI

IG: @donbum2004 | FB: Obumneme Akunyili | LinkedIn: Obumneme Akunyili

College Football

Senior Special Assistant to the Governor of Nigeria's Anambra State

GROWTH

Myfitnesspal.com

I had to re-evaluate my food choices based on my new activity level. It was earth shattering to realize I couldn't still eat two steaks and wash them down with Gatorade at every meal.

GUIDANCE

Learn something new every day. It is never too late to discover a new passion.

EXPERT TO NOVICE

Seriously, when you start a new job, just focus on learning. I didn't know a damn thing when I started; and almost every other person around me walked in with no clue what they were doing either.

SHANNON BAHRKE

IG: @shannonbahrke | FB: Shannon B Happe | shannonbahrke.com & teamempowerhour.com

A three-time US Olympian, Shannon won a silver medal in 2002 and a bronze medal in 2010. She was a member of six World Championship Teams and the US Freestyle Ski Team from 1998-2010. In 2017, Shannon founded Team Empower Hour, a corporate team building company that employs newly-retired Olympians and Olympic hopefuls alike.

ROUTINE

Make time in your day to fulfill your athlete side. I start each day with an hour of exercise and then I move on to growing my company. We've spent so much time putting our bodies first, we must continue to exercise to be successful out of sport. Set a goal like running a marathon, completing a Tough Mudder, or biking 100 miles. Then you can set your sights on conquering the business world.

INSPIRATION

You are NOT alone! Every athlete goes through this difficult transition. The more authentic you are, the more others will go out of their way to help you.

"THE HARD DAYS ARE THE BEST DAYS BECAUSE THAT'S WHEN CHAMPIONS ARE MADE!"
GABBY DOUGLAS

CHALLENGE

What are the 3 most important areas of your life and how can you be successful in ALL of them?

I stay focused on what I want to achieve by keeping my priorities in order:

1. Family

2. Health & wellness

3. Business success

When I first retired, I achieved business success, but completely at the cost of my family and my health. My husband and I were on the brink of divorce. I was working so hard, not exercising enough, constantly sick, and my anxiety was through the roof.

Once I put my family and health back in balance, I found myself much happier. My #3 is sometimes a little slower than I would like, but I know I'm spending every day putting the things I'm most passionate about first.

LESSON

Meaningful connections help define success, and I let too many slip away. I didn't make the effort necessary to ensure lasting friendships with people who supported me along the way. I thought they would always remember me based on my skiing talent. Boy, was that egotistical!

Looking back, I would have better nourished those relationships by letting them know how thankful I was for their support.

EXPERT TO NOVICE

Asking for help is still a challenge for me. When we are athletes, trained professionals give us expert advice all day long. In the business world, we have to seek it out. If you simply ask, you will be surprised by how many people are willing to help.

VINCE POSCENTE

IG: @vinceposcente | Twitter: @vinceposcente | LinkedIn: Vince Poscente | vinceposcente.com

A speed skier, he represented Canada at the 1992 Olympic Winter Games in Albertville, France. Vince is a five-time Canadian record holder and one of only four people inducted into the US and Canadian Speakers' Hall of Fame. He is also an avid mountain climber, participating in seven Himalayan expeditions. Today, Vince is a *New York Times* best-selling Author and works as a Motivational Keynote Speaker with companies including IBM, Merrill Lynch, and American Airlines.

LESSON

You never get to your goal alone. Surround yourself with people smarter than you.

GROWTH

QuickBooks: this app put my bookkeeper out of a job and me in control of my numbers. It's financial accounting at my fingertips.

ROUTINE

Start with your M.I.T's (Most Important Tasks) for success in your routine. This helps me get stuff done without over-scheduling my day. I found this advice from entrepreneurial superstar Peter Thomas, founder of Century 21 Real Estate in Canada.

INSPIRATION

My transition after skiing was brutal. I was depressed and lost. No matter what kind of stud you were as an athlete, we are all fragile.

Stay curious. Keep opening doors. You will find a new path.

PREPARATION

I only had ONE plan: win Olympic gold then become a motivational speaker. But I lost. I placed 15th.

It turns out there is no demand in the speaking business for Olympians who lose.

What would I do differently? Nothing. I had to innovate and be damn good on stage. Necessity is the mother of invention.

GUIDANCE

Seek the path that scares you. If it scares you, it must be important to you. Go towards your fear.

RESOURCES

The War of Art by Steven Pressfield.

The Power of Your Subconscious Mind by Joseph Murphy.

Heck, I'd recommend my book *The Ant and the Elephant,* to learn five action steps to take you to where you are meant to be.

EXPERT TO NOVICE

I assumed that because I was a great athlete, I would be great at my new thing. I was WRONG! You have to start from the beginning and grow from there. Period.

"THE BEST TIME TO FIX A LEAKY ROOF
IS WHEN THE SUN IS SHINING."
JOHN F. KENNEDY

COLIN KASSEKERT

College Baseball
Business Consultant

GUIDANCE

I think a job in sales is a great transition for athletes because of the clear goals and competitive nature. It is also one of the highest paid occupations in the US. We all love a scoreboard!

"WHEN YOU COME TO A FORK IN THE ROAD, TAKE IT."
YOGI BERRA

RICH "BIG DADDY" SALGADO

IG: big_daddy_insures | FB: Richard M Salgado | coastaladvicorsllc.com

College Football
CEO, Coastal Advisors LLC Insurance Consultants

ROUTINE

It's all about getting up and getting moving early. I like to work out at 5 a.m., then take on the day.

"EVERYONE WANTS TO WIN, BUT NOT EVERYONE IS WILLING TO WORK TO WIN."
VINCE LOMBARDI

DR. CAROLINE SILBY

Twitter: @DrSilby | FB: Caroline Silby
| LinkedIn: Caroline Silby | drsilby.
com

Dr. Silby was a member of the National Figure Skating Team and later served on the US Figure Skating Association Board of Directors. A nationally renowned expert in Sport Psychology, she serves as a consultant to Team USA & D.C. United Development Academy. Dr. Silby continues to teach and practice Sport Psychology, and serves on the Board of Directors of several foundations.

INSPIRATION

During your athletic career, it was beneficial to bury your head in your sport. Transitioning is the opposite. You are REBORN. Go CONNECT with people. For the first time in your life, you will discover that your purpose is not tied to a stopwatch or scoreboard.

RESOURCES

Women in the Game Conference is sponsored by USA Basketball. The aim is to educate high school girls, college-aged women, and young professionals on the many career paths that exist in the sports industry.

CHALLENGE

Beyond birth and death, transitioning out of sport is perhaps the most significant change athletes will face. There is a greater risk of developing anxiety or depression during this time period.

"WE DO NOT IMPROVE PERFORMANCE BY CHANGING WHO WE ARE. WE REACH OUR PERFORMANCE PEAK BY MAKING THE MOST OF WHO WE ARE."

Some athletes look forward to having what they call a "normal" life. This includes being free of the pressures and expectations of performance. Yet, when athletes have that freedom, they often find it completely unfamiliar and uncomfortable.

Female athletes universally struggle with post-sport body image, eating patterns, and creating new definitions of health and wellness. Caring for one's body after sport has a different set of rules from pushing one's body to its physical limits.

MENTOR

1. Expose yourself to a broad range of leaders and leadership styles by volunteering for specific people or organizations.

2. If someone offers you help, be prepared to tell them what you need.

3. Continue to follow-up with the mentor, letting the mentor know what you are up to and how their guidance has impacted your choices.

4. Pay it forward and bring people with you on your way up!

PREPARATION

Start thinking about opportunities. You weren't a passive participant in your athletic career. Don't expect to passively transition out of sport either. Like any change, the path ahead includes both the familiar and the unknown. It may feel scary, but as elite athletes you have already successfully faced similar unknowns.

SUPPORT

Given there are few 50 year-old figure skaters or track stars, every athlete will come to a point of transition. While no two athletes will take the same path, connecting with people who understand the athlete transition can provide comfort during a confusing time.

PAUL HARTZELL

A professional baseball player, Paul was drafted by the California Angels in 1975. He pitched in the MLB for the Angels, Twins, Orioles, and Brewers from 1976-1984. Post-sports, he founded Blockchain Integrated Partners and serves on the board for Game Plan, a career and mentor marketplace for athletes. Today, Paul works for Carbonite as the Microsoft Alliance Manager.

INSPIRATION

Think back to how little you knew when you started your sports career. Now think of learning something new in the same way. Don't be embarrassed to ask for help from colleagues, bosses, or other people in the industry who have been successful.

PREPARATION

I see learning as a lifelong process. While I was a professional athlete, I took courses at the University of California, Irvine. It was challenging, but my degree in Mechanical Engineering prepared me for almost anything.

RESOURCES

I am very partial to Game Plan, a company at which I serve on the board of directors (wearegameplan.com). Game Plan helps athletic organizations support their athletes through online education, mentorship, and career services. They're doing fantastic work in the NBA G League, USA Basketball, and about 60 colleges and universities.

LESSON

Your biggest defeat will be quickly forgotten by most people. As difficult as it seems, turn the page. Get up off the ground, dust yourself off, and keep working hard.

"IF YOU DON'T HAVE TIME TO DO IT RIGHT, WHEN WILL YOU HAVE TIME TO DO IT OVER?"
JOHN WOODEN

NATIONAL CHAMPION

JADE PERRY

IG: @jpizzle55 | Twitter: @coachjadeperry55 | FB: Jade Perry

A three-time All-American basketball player at Muhlenberg North in Greenville, KY. Jade went on to win the NCAA Division I Women's Basketball National Championship in 2006. She played in 139 games during her collegiate career, grabbing more than 700 rebounds. Today, Jade is the Head Women's Basketball Coach at SUNY Canton.

LESSON

Accountability. Being properly prepared and on-time are vital traits for success in whatever comes next.

GUIDANCE

Give yourself options! Sometimes life throws curveballs and it doesn't go as you hoped — have a Plan A, Plan B, and Plan C.

RESOURCES

Post Moves by Angela Lewis. I highly recommend this book for female athletes navigating the transition from sports to the real world.

CHALLENGE

In April 2008, I watched as two of my teammates were drafted and my name was never called. The WNBA had been my dream since I was nine years old. Basketball was all I knew, and I was lost.

Later that year, I failed a class and wasn't able to graduate with my teammates. I had to go to summer school. When I missed the first day of class, my head coach called and told me that not getting my degree would make me a failure in life, but she promised to help me if I applied myself. It was just what I needed to hear.

The following semester, I completed my Bachelors' Degree. My head coach kept her promise. I'm now a college basketball coach and an academic advisor. Giving back and living that purpose driven life is the most rewarding experience.

"IT DOESN'T MATTER WHO YOU ARE, OR WHERE YOU'RE FROM. ANYTHING IS POSSIBLE IF YOU HAVE A DREAM AND KEEP GOD FIRST."
REVEREND OTIS CUNNINGHAM

RICK COSTA JR.

IG: @rcosta4343

College Football
Psychologist

ROUTINE

We are a product of our most consistent actions. I start each day by seeking some small sense of accomplishment. I do 100 push-ups and 100 crunches before leaving the house.

Each morning, I practice techniques associated with Neuro Linguistic Programming (NLP). Here's how it works:

I write five "I am" statements regarding what I specifically want to accomplish in the coming weeks, months, and years. Then, I enthusiastically read them aloud 5 consecutive times and record it on my phone. I play this recording on a loop while brushing my teeth.

Rather than allowing random thoughts to take over, I find this helps me to focus. We are all being conditioned by various aspects of our environment on a regular basis. I prefer greater control over my own mental and emotional well-being.

"EVEN IF YOU ARE ON THE RIGHT TRACK, YOU WILL
GET RUN OVER IF YOU JUST SIT THERE."
WILL ROGERS

BILL CLEMENT

IG: @billclement10 | Twitter: @billclement10 | FB: Bill Clement | LinkedIn: Bill Clement | billclementspeaking.com

A two-time Stanley Cup Champion with the Philadelphia Flyers, Bill spent 11 seasons in the National Hockey League. He was named Team Captain for the Washington Capitals, and earned two All-Star appearances. After retirement, Bill worked as a Color Commentator for ESPN, ABC, and NBC, including five Olympic Games. In his 2013 TEDx Talk: *Success: Nature or Nurture?,* he discusses the origins of success. Today, Bill continues his work behind the mic as a Professional Speaker and Broadcaster.

LESSON

The world doesn't care how many times you get knocked down — only how many times you get back up. Tenacity and persistence are important qualities.

ROUTINE

First step? Get up at the same time every day and make exercise a priority. It doesn't matter what kind it is. These acts start a process of developing time management skills and discipline.

> "TO THE WORLD YOU MAY JUST BE ONE PERSON,
> BUT TO ONE PERSON, YOU MAY BE THE WORLD."
> DR. SEUSS

INSPIRATION

If you are struggling, then start helping other people; as many as you can. Set weekly goals for the number of acts of help you would like to achieve. You will see life through a different lens.

FAILURE

I overcame corporate and personal bankruptcy two years after I retired.

I jumped into the restaurant franchising business by purchasing the rights to a Canadian bakery-deli chain. The plan was to open a flagship store, sell franchises, and ultimately ride off into the restaurant franchising sunset. Instead, I lost nearly everything. At age 34, I was broke, scared, and depressed. To compound my situation, I had no income, no job, no career-training or college degree. I had attacked the restaurant business with the same intensity I had used as an athlete. Little did I know, intensity alone would not work. I had failed for the first time in my life.

I believe that success is built on two things that must be earned; trust and respect. The only thing I truly owned was my credibility, so I set out to rebuild it and it slowly worked. Whenever I am asked about this time in my life, I always answer that I owe EVERY success in my post-hockey life to my greatest failure. While it was painful to go through, it was invaluable on so many levels and I shudder to think of what life would be like had I not failed.

RESOURCES

Think and Grow Rich by Napoleon Hill.

CARYN DAVIES

IG: @carynpdavies | Twitter: @carynpdavies | FB: Caryn Davies | LinkedIn: Caryn Davies | caryndavies.com

Caryn won gold at the 2008 and 2012 Summer Olympic Games in Women's Eight Rowing. She has won more Olympic medals than any other US oarswoman. In 2013, Caryn was inducted into the New York Athletic Club Hall of Fame. She holds an undergraduate degree from Harvard, a J.D. from Columbia Law School, and an MBA from Oxford University. Today, Caryn works as a Lawyer for Goodwin Procter in Boston, MA.

ROUTINE

I focus on efficient time management. When I was training for the Olympics, my life was simple. I could distill it down to one goal. My routine was completely designed around accomplishing that one goal.

After retiring, suddenly I had multiple goals: career, fitness, family, friends, and hobbies. If I wanted to fit them all in, then I had to look for the synergies and create efficiencies. That takes planning ahead.

INSPIRATION

Maintaining structure will help you maintain your sanity.

"WHAT YOU ARE IN LOVE WITH, WHAT
SEIZES YOUR IMAGINATION, WILL
AFFECT EVERYTHING."

ATTRIBUTED TO FR. PEDRO ARRUPE

CHALLENGE

I've struggled with defining clear and visible metrics for measuring success.

As an oarswoman, it was clear who was performing and who wasn't. I kept my head down, worked hard, and let my performance speak for itself.

As a lawyer, my colleagues can't see whether or not I'm doing good work. I've had to learn how to advocate for myself and tout my successes in order to advance in my career.

PREPARATION

I went to law school while I trained for the Olympics. In fact, I was filling out clerkship applications from my room at the Olympic Village in London. And I got the job!

EXPERT TO NOVICE

It's hard to go from the pinnacle of one pursuit to the bottom of another. When you're starting at the bottom, you need a singular focus on the path ahead.

ATTOLLO

JORDAN STEFFY

IG: @jordan_steffy | FB: Jordan Steffy | LinkedIn: Jordan Steffy | attolloprep.org

College Football

CEO, Attollo Prep / Founder, Children Deserve a Chance Foundation

MENTOR

Find a way to add value to your mentor. Once the relationship goes from being one-sided to mutually beneficial, you'll have created something that will last.

PREPARATION

I maximized my status as an athlete to get meetings with influencers in the area and took advantage of networking opportunities on campus. I looked at every interaction as an investment that could pay dividends in the future. This has led to many friendships that are still fruitful over a decade later.

"YOU SHOULD TEACH SOMETHING SHORTLY AFTER YOU LEARNED IT, WHILE YOU STILL REMEMBER WHAT IT'S LIKE TO NOT KNOW IT."

FAILURE

My college football career didn't live up to my expectations. When I reflected on the things that were within my control, I was forced to acknowledge that I made many decisions based on fear.

I learned that preparation can help mitigate this anxiety, and that gratitude and fear cannot coexist. This has dramatically changed the way I've approached the next phases of my life.

RESOURCES

Podcasts:

The Tim Ferriss Show by Tim Ferriss.

Master of Scale by Reid Hoffman.

Books:

Outliers by Malcolm Gladwell: making sense of greatness, and how people become extraordinary.

The Power of Moments by Chip and Dan Heath: creating meaningful experiences.

Eleven Rings by Phil Jackson: the power of leadership and how to build teams.

BONNIE BLAIR CRUIKSHANK

IG: @bonnieblairc | Twitter: @bonnieblair | LinkedIn: Bonnie Blair Cruikshank

A six-time Olympic medalist in speed skating, Bonnie is one of the most decorated women in US Winter Olympic history. Today, Bonnie works as a Motivational Speaker.

LESSON

Never say never. You won't know how far you can go until you try. You just have to set your mind and body to it.

DOUGLAS CLARK LENNOX II

Olympic Swimming
Assistant Swimming Coach, Princeton University

CHALLENGE

It's easy to confuse your competitive accomplishments with your identity. When sport ends, you have to mentally and emotionally reset.

Becoming elite at what you do takes time. I was a swimmer for 20 years. It's unreasonable to expect to master anything until you have invested the time, energy, and effort.

"THE DAY OF THE RACE IS TOO
LATE TO WANT TO WIN."

LESSON

Just because you used to be good at something doesn't mean you will stay good unless you continue to put in the work. There is no such thing as staying the same. You're either getting better or worse! Everything you do in life requires constant training.

PIERRE BANKS

IG: @pierrembanks | Twitter: @pierrembanks | FB: Pierre Banks | LinkedIn: Pierre Banks | banksboy.com

College Football

Director of Student-Athlete Development, Appalachian State University

CHALLENGE

Understand that being an athlete is just one of the seasons in your life. Building a strong foundation of self makes the transition easier. Who you are doesn't change, it's only the season that changes.

"'LOVE THE LORD YOUR GOD WITH ALL YOUR HEART, ALL YOUR SOUL, ALL YOUR STRENGTH, AND ALL YOUR MIND'; AND, 'LOVE YOUR NEIGHBOR AS YOURSELF.'"

LUKE 10:27; LEVITICUS 19:18

TOM BILLUPS

FB: Tom Billups | LinkedIn: Tom Billups

A rugby player, Tom had a decade-long career, including 44 career international appearances. He played in the 1999 Rugby World Cup and was the National Team Head Coach at the 2003 Rugby World Cup. In 2015, Tom was inducted into the US Rugby Hall of Fame. In 2018, he became the 14th recipient of the Craig Sweeney Award, presented for contributions to the sport and exemplary character. Today, Tom serves as Associate Head Coach for the rugby program at the University of California, Berkeley.

INSPIRATION

When the sport is no longer what you do, who you are as a person will matter most. Be known by your deeds as a person, not just as an athlete performing on the field.

PREPARATION

I began preparing during my last two seasons as a player by keeping a journal of all the things I would and wouldn't do if I ever became a coach.

GUIDANCE

Begin by understanding your strengths and don't be afraid to exploit them. Whether it be selling a product or providing a service, the ability to connect with people and communicate clearly is important.

RESOURCES

Warfighting by U.S. Marine Corps Staff.

LESSON

Sports taught me:

1. I had control over the amount of effort and focus I put into preparing.

2. I had control over how I responded when results did or didn't go my way.

3. The richest experiences come from being on a team.

PAUL VADEN

IG: @paul_vaden | Twitter: @answerthebell | FB: Paul Vaden | LinkedIn: Paul Vaden | answerthebell.com

A boxer known as "The Ultimate," Paul won the US amateur Light Middleweight championship in 1990. In 1995, he won the IBF World Light Middleweight title as a professional. Paul is the author of *Answer the Bell: Inventing Your Life as a Champion.* His "Answer the Bell" program advocates for the importance of stress management and a balanced lifestyle. Today, Paul is a Speaker, Consultant, and documentary Filmmaker.

MENTOR

Find someone who's not only been successful, but has also been battle tested. Someone who's had to get up off the canvas and made it through to the other side. A great mentee is full of questions and listens. Be a sponge.

GUIDANCE

Make sure you find a genuine passion. Something that vibrates your soul. Make sure you're not doing it for your parents, or bragging rights, or to be liked by others. Live out YOUR script.

"SERVICE TO OTHERS IS THE RENT YOU
PAY FOR YOUR ROOM HERE ON EARTH."

MUHAMMAD ALI

RESOURCES

Answer the Bell: Inventing Your Life as a Champion by Paul Vaden.

PREPARATION

During my boxing career, I developed a network of professional contacts that set the stage for my post-athletic career success.

LESSON

You're not going to win every round in athletics or life. But you should work hard enough to win each round. Resiliency, discipline, adaptation and stamina are tools elite athletes can draw on to overcome any challenges.

SHAUNA ROHBOCK

A professional soccer player for the San Diego Spirit of the WUSA. Shauna went on to become an Olympic bobsledder, winning a silver medal at the 2006 Winter Games. In 2018, she was appointed to the President's Council on Sports, Fitness & Nutrition. Today, Shauna works as a Bobsled Coach and a Soldier in the US Army National Guard.

ROUTINE

Athletes don't plan one day at a time when competing. We plan months ahead of time. As you transition from sports, your process of preparation shouldn't change. Setting short and long-term goals for yourself gives you a direction. Try and plan out as far as you can. This way you can prepare for what is ahead.

INSPIRATION

You didn't become an elite athlete overnight, and you won't become an everyday person overnight either.

CHRIS TURNER

IG: @JuneChris I FB: Chris Turner

College Football

Manager, Möet Hennessy

GROWTH

I consume news, pop culture, history and philosophy. Anything to expand the mind. One of my favorite apps is *Waking Up with Sam Harris*.

ROUTINE

Time management, punctuality, and personal accountability separate you from your peers.

"WE DIDN'T LOSE, WE JUST RAN OUT OF TIME."
VINCE LOMBARDI

PREPARATION

I wish someone would have sat me down and highlighted the importance of financial literacy. That said, it's also important to have fun and splurge on experiences. Find a balance.

RESOURCES

History lessons are always grounding. Think it's hard finding a job? Try planning the D-Day invasion. Heartbroken from a breakup? Try losing a child in a mass shooting. The point isn't to minimize one's own struggles, but to gain insight and perspective from others throughout history.

LESSON

We are incredibly lucky people to have had the opportunity to experience something that most people on this planet have not. The transition is difficult, but I wouldn't trade a single second of it for anything. I think about my team-mates every day. I think about my coaches every day. I think about the big wins and crushing defeats every day. I wouldn't be who I am today otherwise.

DR. RICHARD COSTA

Professional Bodybuilder
Medical Doctor

LESSON

In 1972, I had the privilege of sparring with Muhammad Ali for one round. The humility he showed by treating everyone in the gym like an individual would stick with me forever. I took that lesson into my professional career and it still influences how I interact with my patients today.

PREPARATION

There was no time to rest when I was competing professionally, studying to enter medical school, and working full-time at my health food store. I read my medical books between sets at the gym and between customers at the store. Do what you have to do to get the job done.

GROWTH

The Story of My Experiments With Truth by Mohandas Gandhi.

Zen and the Art of Motorcycle Maintenance by Robert Pirsig. This book taught me to leave the past behind and that the ingredients for success lie not in the final destination, but along the journey.

INSPIRATION

Live each day as if it's your last. It's better to have tried and failed, than to have never tried at all.

"THE KEY TO SUCCESS IS TO KEEP GROWING IN ALL AREAS: MENTAL, EMOTIONAL, SPIRITUAL, AND PHYSICAL."

ALONZO JONES

LinkedIn: Alonzo Jones

Mr. Jones is the Associate Athletic Director for Championship Life at Arizona State University. In his 2016 TEDx Talk: *The Situational Identity Matrix*, he shares unique insight on athletes and the life situations they encounter. Today, Mr. Jones also works as an Author and Professional Speaker.

PREPARATION

A young person walks up to a refrigerator and thinks, *hmmm, what can I take out?* A grown-minded person walks up to a refrigerator and thinks, *hmmm, what do I need to put in it?*

You have to get your mind right.

For athletes, tangibly, this means a devoted number of hours per week to learning. Not begrudged learning, but open and scholarly learning. I encourage you to approach texts and subjects with the purpose to permanently remember what you are learning so that you can call upon it in the future. All future decisions are made by pulling from what you already know.

RESOURCES

45 - The Warrior Class by Alonzo Jones. A book on College Men - Students and Student-Athletes and the Timeless Quest for Sexual Conquest.

"EVERYBODY CAN BE GREAT, BECAUSE
ANYBODY CAN SERVE."

DR. MARTIN LUTHER KING JR.

TOM "TONY" RICCA

IG: @tonyriccawwe | Twitter: @tonyriccawwe | FB: Tony Ricca WWE | LinkedIn: Tony Ricca WWE | tonyricca.com

Professional Wrestler

CEO, Showtime Wrestling

INSPIRATION

Many opportunities present themselves to those who look through the smallest lens.

LESSON

Don't abandon the principles that have helped you along the way. Stay organized and focus on the task.

"THE SKY IS LIMITLESS."

KATIE
O'DONNELL BAM

IG: @katieod16 |
Twitter: @katieodonnellfh |
katieodonnellfh.com

A field hockey player, Katie was a four-time All-American and two-time US Olympian. She won the 2009 National Player of the Year Award, followed by the National Sportswoman of the Year Award in 2010. Katie's National Teams won the gold medal at the 2011 and 2015 Pan-American Games. In 2013, she signed an agreement to represent and advise on products for the field hockey manufacturer STX. Today, Katie is an Assistant Women's Field Hockey Coach at her alma mater.

ROUTINE

When I was fresh out of sport, the freedom of creating my own schedule was awesome. After a month, when my mental vacation ended, I missed having someone tell me where to be and what to do.

When a coach or trainer tells you to work out, you HAVE to do it.

When YOU set your schedule, it's easy to think, *I'll do it later. Why am I doing this now?*

My advice is to make goals and stick to them because they're important to YOU. Trust me when I say, this is easier said than done. I'm two years out and still working on this. But as times goes by, it does become easier.

INSPIRATION

You've spent years perfecting your sport, now spend time finding new ways to fill your heart. Recently I heard Tori McClure, the first woman to row solo across the Atlantic Ocean, say, "Life's too short to only learn from your mistakes, so learn from others too."

PREPARATION

I wouldn't have done anything differently. I had no idea what I wanted to do in life, so I took a coaching job while considering my options. This offered me time to learn about other things that piqued my interest. In the process of searching for my future career, I fell in love with coaching.

LESSON

The details matter in anything you choose to do. If you give half, you get half. Pay attention, follow through on the details, and complete your mission like it's the Olympic Games! You will encounter people who have no idea what it takes to be successful. Educate them instead of letting them frustrate you.

"EVERYDAY IS A CHOICE. CHOOSE LOVE,
CHOOSE HAPPINESS, DON'T COMPLAIN.
CHOOSE TO SEE THE GOOD."
KATIE O'DONNELL BAM

JAMES TOWNSEND

IG: @youngtonym | FB: James Townsend

College Football

Gym Owner, The Brave One Gym

INSPIRATION

Be patient. Sort out your options, then grind your way to the top. Make yourself and those around you proud.

"I WILL NEVER LEAVE YOU NOR FORSAKE YOU."
HEBREWS 13:5

CHRIS GOLD

FB: Christopher Gold

College Golfer

Professional Golf Caddy

INSPIRATION

Have a plan for every day. Every day you don't practice, someone else is getting better, smarter, and learning more by working harder. No days off.

BRANDON ELLIS

College Football
College Athletics Administrator

PREPARATION

During college, internships are key. Take advantage of gaining real life experience in industries you may want to work in.

RESOURCES

Good to Great by Jim Collins. A must read for those interested in management.

EXPERT TO NOVICE

My transition took a while. It really happened over time and through self-reflection.

My biggest challenge was adapting to a new environment. When I entered Corporate America working for Johnson & Johnson, I was not the highly touted recruit from Lafayette College anymore. I had to channel the same competitive drive which allowed me to excel on the field and bring that over into the business world.

JANINE SHEPHERD

IG: @janine_shepherd | Twitter: @janineshepherd | FB: Janine Shepherd Author | LinkedIn: Janine Shepherd | janineshepherd.com

A champion cross-country skier and member of the Australian Olympic Team. In her TEDx Talk: *A Broken Body Isn't a Broken Person*, Janine shares her story about the accident that changed her life. She has written six best-selling books, including her newly released memoir, *Defiant*. Today, Janine works as an Author and Professional Speaker.

ROUTINE

My morning routine sets the direction for the rest of my day. I start by giving thanks. Gratitude puts me in the right mindset and helps me maintain a positive outlook all day.

INSPIRATION

Always stay close to the things that uplift and inspire you.

LESSON

As a young athlete, I taught myself to love training on the hills when many of my teammates took the flat course. This was my edge! This not only gave me physical strength, but also mental stamina. The hills are the things we don't necessarily like in our lives, but when we learn to love them, anything is possible.

"LOVE THE HILLS."
JANINE SHEPHERD

PATRICK J. SWEENEY II

IG: @TheFearGuru | Twitter: @PJSweeney | FB: Patrick Sweeney Fear Guru | LinkedIn: Patrick J Sweeney II | pjsweeney.com

Three-time World Cup Rower and 2nd in the US Olympic Trials in the single scull. Patrick won the 2018 Race Across America, was first to cycle Everest Base Camp, the summit of Kilimanjaro, and Mount Elbrus. Today, he works as a TV Host, Tech Entrepreneur, and Motivational Speaker.

GROWTH

CogniFit: a brain training app that keeps the neuroplasticity of the brain growing at any age. I never would have thought my brain needed training. Now, I find it just as important as training my body.

ROUTINE

I start my day by practicing meditation and breathing — then I workout. I write down the top three things I want to accomplish that day and take a cold shower before work. Find a daily routine that works for you.

INSPIRATION

Winning is the greatest feeling in the world. For many athletes, the first taste is during competition. Look for a career that allows you this same addictive feeling. It could be anything from closing a sales deal to releasing a new product, or writing amazing code.

"IT'S NOT THE CRITIC WHO COUNTS: NOT THE MAN WHO POINTS OUT HOW THE STRONG MAN STUMBLES, OR WHERE THE DOER OF DEEDS COULD HAVE DONE THEM BETTER. THE CREDIT BELONGS TO THE MAN WHO IS ACTUALLY IN THE ARENA, WHOSE FACE IS MARRED BY DUST AND SWEAT AND BLOOD; WHO STRIVES VALIANTLY; WHO ERRS, WHO COMES SHORT AGAIN AND AGAIN, BE-CAUSE THERE IS NO EFFORT WITHOUT ERROR AND SHORTCOMING."

THEODORE ROOSEVELT

PREPARATION

My mindset has always been – I might not be great now, but I know how to become great at anything.

RESOURCES

Confessions of an S.O.B. by Al Neuharth.

Fear is Fuel by Patrick Sweeney. Learn to use fear as the ultimate performance enhancer.

LESSON

Accountability. Too many people play the victim. They're late for an interview and they blame traffic. A bad review and they blame their boss. When you are a victim, life is happening to you. Take control and become the author of your world.

BALIAN BUSCHBAUM

IG: @buschbaumbalian | FB: Balian
Buschbaum | LinkedIn: Balian
Buschbaum | balian-buschbaum.de

An Olympic pole vaulter representing Germany, formerly known as
Yvonne Buschbaum. Balian won a gold medal at the 1999 European
Junior Championships and placed sixth in the women's pole vault at
the 2000 Olympic Games in Sydney. A celebrity LGBT advocate, today
Balian works as an Author and Inspirational Speaker.

INSPIRATION

Know who you are. Keep your head up. There is always a way.

GUIDANCE

It's simple. Follow your heart.

LESSON

I think it's really important to be authentic. I would like to see a world where
athletes no longer have to endure discrimination, obvious or hidden.

"THE PATH TO FREEDOM IS COURAGE."

MARK HALL

IG: @ mark__a__hall | FB: Mark Hall

College Football

Corporate Trainer, Pharmaceutical Industry

ROUTINE

The loss of routine was probably the hardest thing to overcome. My solution has been to write a detailed plan with specific goals and stick to it. This makes it easier to stay on track.

MENTOR

Seek out more than one mentor. Each has unique experiences to share. This allows you to learn best practices from a wide range of leaders.

LESSON

Sports taught me how to work hard. When you're the hardest worker in the room it builds trust and offers credibility when you bring ideas to the table.

BRIAN CRONISE

IG: @croniseb | Twitter: @croniseb

College Lacrosse & Diving

Financial Technology Consultant

ROUTINE

Set a goal to participate in an activity that takes structure to train for – a triathlon, half marathon, or FULL marathon! Not only will you stay in shape, but it will give you something to look forward to after work.

"THE BEST WAY OUT IS ALWAYS THROUGH."
ROBERT FROST

KIKKAN RANDALL

IG: @kikkanimal | Twitter: @kikkanimal | FB: Kikkan Randall | LinkedIn: Kikkan Randall | kikkan.com

A five-time Olympian, Kikkan won a gold medal in cross-country skiing at the 2018 Winter Olympics in South Korea. Her career includes 17 US National titles, 29 World Cup podiums and World Championship Medals. Kikkan was inducted into the Alaska Sports Hall of Fame in 2011. Today, she serves on the IOC's Athletes Commission, as President of Fast and Female USA, and Brand Ambassador for L.L. Bean.

ROUTINE

At the end of the day I rate myself on how productive I was, similar to how I used to record my training in a training log. I've found evaluating my progress every day gives me the mental boost that I used to get from completing training sessions.

INSPIRATION

Your athletic career wasn't built in a day. Have patience and work on accomplishing small goals. Soon you will build your new normal and discover your new identity.

MENTOR

Sometimes the hardest part is getting up the courage to ask someone if they would share their experience. I've found most people are totally open to it and are happy to pass along what they've learned.

To be a good mentee, you want to be open-minded, curious, and prepared. You demonstrate your willingness to learn by putting in the work.

CHALLENGE

Negative body image is a huge obstacle to overcome for many athletes. As an athlete, you trained your body to be in top shape. You felt strong. You felt fit. You felt confident. But, the body is bound to change when you're not training at that same high level anymore.

Once sport ends, you have to mentally let go of what you used to be able to do. Setting new goals is an important first step.

SUPPORT

I've found it beneficial to stay connected with former teammates and competitors through social media. It takes effort since we don't see each other at training and races anymore. But, it's been worth the effort!

I reach out to my sport friends not only when it's going well, but also when I am struggling. Having a support system of people who are going through the same challenges has been helpful.

JAY WEISS

Twitter: @jtwcoach

A four-year varsity wrestler at Franklin & Marshall. Since 1994, Jay has led the Harvard University wrestling program, serving as Head Coach. He is a two-time Eastern Intercollegiate Wrestling Association Coach of the Year award winner, mentoring two national champions, 17 EIWA champions and 19 All-Americans.

ROUTINE

Wake up early. Be organized with your time.

I feel the routine an athlete develops during their competitive career serves as a great foundation for creating a successful routine later in life. I try not to manage my athletes' schedules too much. This way they know how to better manage themselves after sports.

CHALLENGE

Character is revealed in the ways we handle adversity and success. I constantly remind my student-athletes that their identity is NOT tied to their successes on the mat, rather the character they've developed throughout the journey. When we give maximum effort without worrying about outcome, we are much better off.

GUIDANCE

Finding your "why" isn't easy. But it's easier to find when you're chasing your passion.

Find something that will impact others. And make sure you laugh every day.

RESOURCES

The Alchemist by Paulo Coelho.

Man's Search for Meaning by Viktor Frankl.

"INVEST IN RELATIONSHIPS NOT BECAUSE YOU WANT SOMETHING, BUT BECAUSE YOU WANT TO BUILD SOMETHING."

JON GORDON

DERECK FAULKNER

IG: @dereckfaulkner | Twitter: @dereckfaulkner | FB: Dereck Faulkner

Professional Football

Non-Profit Executive Director / Corporate Business and Marketing Manager

GUIDANCE

Athletes should engage themselves in communities unrelated to sports. Finding mentors and professionals in different industries will offer a broader understanding of transitional steps.

RESOURCES

Unlabel: Selling You Without Selling Out by Marc Ecko.

DR. JUDY L. VAN RAALTE

A Professor of Psychology at Springfield College and Certified Mental Performance Coach. Dr. Van Raalte is a member of the US Olympic Committee Registry for sport psychologists and has presented at conferences in 18 countries. Her research has been funded by the National Institute of Mental Health, the NCAA, and the International Tennis Federation.

INSPIRATION

You are a workplace asset because you were an athlete. The communication, leadership, and problem-solving skills you've developed in sport are strengths on the job market.

PREPARATION

Create a resume. Applying for jobs is easier when you already have a head start.

FORESIGHT

Many athletes think that they have to have everything figured out right away. Take time to explore your options. It is OK to change directions as you search for your post-sports career fit.

RESOURCES

Athlete's Guide to Career Planning by Petitpas, Champagne, Chartrand, Danish, and Murphy.

The NCAA funds free evidence-based career information at supportforsport.org.

MICKEY FEIN

IG: @coachfein | Twitter: @micfein

College Basketball and Football

College Football Coach

LESSON

Being on time, working hard, and being prepared are things that make me successful to this day.

> "HARD WORK BEATS TALENT WHEN TALENT DOESN'T WORK."

DAVID HOLLOWAY

IG: @dxholloway | FB: David Alexander Holloway | LinkedIn: David Holloway | davidholloway.com

Professional Football

Motivational Speaker

FAILURE

Replacing FAILURE with LESSON is a great skill to practice. These lessons have proven to be great teachers.

RESOURCES

How to Argue and Win Every Time by Gerry Spence.

> "WITH A VISION OF GREATNESS, ANYTHING IS POSSIBLE."

WILLIAM HESMER

IG: @williamhesmer | Twitter: @williamhesmer | FB: William Hesmer | LinkedIn: William Hesmer | sportingwealthpartners.com

An All-American soccer player at Wake Forest University, William was drafted 17th overall in the 2004 MLS Draft by the Kansas City Wizards. He enjoyed a nine-year professional career. In 2014, William was inducted into the North Carolina Soccer Hall of Fame. Today, he works in wealth management and is the Founder of Sporting Wealth Partners.

ROUTINE

Time is your most valuable asset. Maximize and protect your time as best you can. Do not waste it, nor let others hijack it.

In order to protect it, you have to learn what YOU want out of your life. Until you know that, it's almost impossible to structure your time effectively.

PREPARATION

The smartest thing I ever did was intern for two years with a financial firm while I was still playing professionally. I don't want to sugar coat it; it was hard to balance my time and to deal with the perception of not being "all-in" as an athlete. However, overcoming these obstacles helped me transition into my next career almost seamlessly.

"CHOOSE A TASK BIG OR SMALL, DO IT RIGHT OR NOT AT ALL."

LESSON

One of my childhood idols was Hall of Fame goalie Tony Meola. As fate would have it, I spent my rookie year as his backup. At the end of the season, I saw how this legend was being "pushed out" of the game. He was completely blindsided when they released him. This always stuck with me and it was why I prepared so diligently for my next step.

RESOURCES

Start With Why by Simon Sinek.

Finding my "why" was the essential ingredient for protecting and maximizing my time. This is a process you cannot rush, so take your time and think it out, even if it takes a few years.

CATRIONA LE MAY DOAN, O.C.

IG: @catrionald | Twitter: @catrionald

Competing in four Olympic Games, Catriona was known as "the fastest woman on ice." A speed skater, she won back-to-back gold medals in the 500m speed skating event. A two-time Canadian flag bearer at the Winter Olympics, Catriona was inducted into the Canadian Sports Hall of Fame in 2008. Today, she works in Community Engagement in Calgary.

INSPIRATION

Results do not dictate the character of an individual. Falling at the 1994 Olympic Games helped me gain perspective and brought me to my faith.

CHALLENGE

Women face different challenges than men after sport. Many female athletes may choose to start a family, which is a completely different set of challenges. Not only physically, but emotionally and socially as well. These challenges are a little less daunting when athletes have a good foundation of who they are pre-family and pre-retirement.

GUIDANCE

Discovering a new passion might not be the most difficult thing, it is accepting it. I think sometimes we have an idea of how things should go, or who we are, and we must keep an open mind.

"I LEARNED THAT COURAGE WAS NOT THE ABSENCE OF FEAR, BUT THE TRIUMPH OVER IT. THE BRAVE MAN IS NOT HE WHO DOES NOT FEEL AFRAID, BUT HE WHO CONQUERS THAT FEAR."

NELSON MANDELA

CHAD LEWIS

IG: @chadlewis89 | Twitter: @chadlewis89 | LinkedIn: Chad Lewis

A Super Bowl champion and three-time Pro Bowl tight end, Chad played in the NFL for the Philadelphia Eagles and St. Louis Rams from 1997-2005. Fluent in Mandarin, Chad served as an NFL Ambassador to Taiwan, Singapore, and Thailand. His memoir, *Surround Yourself With Greatness,* was published in 2009. Today, Chad is an Associate Athletic Director at his alma mater, Brigham Young University.

ROUTINE

As soon as you finish playing, everything changes. It's vital to get into a routine to keep yourself spiritually, physically, financially, socially, and mentally healthy.

Doing two simple things will have an enormous impact on each day moving forward:

1. Read scriptures. This simple act of dedication will bless and reward every part of your life. It doesn't require much time, but will result in subtle blessings. Things will just seem to work better. Your mind will be a little clearer. Your patience for yourself and others will be enlarged.

2. Count your blessings. Think of all the good things you have going for you. There is so much to be thankful for. Our Heavenly Father has blessed us beyond comprehension. When

we acknowledge our blessings, a miraculous thing happens. They start to multiply! This is the same thing that happens when we dwell on our problems. They also multiply. The arithmetic is amazing. Whatever we focus on will grow!

INSPIRATION

Make sure what you consume inspires you to be your best. Surround yourself with greatness and avoid what brings you down.

"LET YOUR LIGHT SHINE."
MATTHEW 5:16

LESSON

Be humble AND hungry. Andy Reid, my former coach, consistently reinforced these two life lessons.

1. Be humble. A new career requires humility since our peers have been in the corporate world for much longer. So what?! We have incredible experience that adds value to organizations way more than we think.

2. Be hungry. Get a job. Even if it is an entry-level position. Don't worry about the salary. That will come. Many former athletes are hesitant to take entry-level jobs because the salary seems so scary low. Instead, they don't take a job until they are completely broke. Get to work. That is number one. Don't work out all day long. Don't do fake stuff. Get a job.

RICHARD DI PIETRO

IG: @Rich_Di_Pietro | Twitter: @Rich_Di_Pietro | FB: Rich Di Pietro | richdipietro.com

College Wrestler

Public Sector Construction / Real Estate Development

GROWTH

I use the *Wall Street Journal* audio edition.

ROUTINE

The biggest staples in my routine are exercise and thoughtful reflection. I do my best thinking at the gym. Each day I consider three key things:

1. What I want to accomplish and why.

2. Lessons learned from recent events and their impact moving forward.

3. A positive experience from the prior day to celebrate small victories.

I find this gives me a healthier and more strategic outlook.

INSPIRATION

Don't be afraid to ask for help. Remember, the game isn't over, it's only changed venues. The keys to success remain the same. Your coaches and teammates still care and want to help you. They merely have different titles now. Sports have not, nor will they ever, define you. You are special, not the jersey you wore.

LESSON

Every success story has one thing in common: they didn't quit. In the face of adversity, they kept moving forward. Success is realized by those who don't give up.

"YOU CAN'T CONTROL WHAT
HAPPENS IN LIFE, BUT YOU CAN
CONTROL HOW YOU REACT."

DR. JOY MACCI

Twitter: @joymacci | FB: Joy Macci |
LinkedIn: Joy Macci PhD | joyofsport.
com & drjoymacci.com

A former professional tennis player, Dr. Macci is a renowned Leadership Coach. She's worked with Olympians and tennis stars including Serena and Venus Williams, Andy Roddick, and Jennifer Capriati. Dr. Macci is the CEO of Joy of Sport, providing "best of the best" in national and international tennis, fitness, and sports management. She is the founding President for UN Women (DFW Chapter - USNC), and an Adjunct Professor at the University of Dallas. Today, Dr. Macci also works as a Professional Speaker and best-selling Author.

FAILURE

Make failure your friend. Failure is never final, unless you allow it to be. Learning from your failure is key to developing the champion in you. As legendary Coach Vince Lombardi once said, "Winners never quit and quitters never win."

INSPIRATION

Keep your faith & focus. Your mastery of athletic skills, disciplines, and strategies can be of great value in the business world. Pick your lane and master it!

SUPPORT

Female athletes can impact each other's success by involving themselves in leadership positions.

After you've successfully transitioned, help inspire the next generation of female athletes by volunteering, coaching, and mentoring at the high school, college, or professional level.

"YOU HAVE TO BELIEVE IN YOURSELF WHEN
NO ONE ELSE DOES. THAT'S WHAT
MAKES YOU A WINNER!"
VENUS WILLIAMS

RAJIV LUNDY

IG: @Rajiv5 | FB: Rajiv Lundy |
LinkedIn: Rajiv Lundy

College Football

Mortgage Servicing / Real Estate Agent

GROWTH

Apps: *TED* (Ted Talks), *CreditKarma, Chakra Meditation*.

INSPIRATION

Stop tweeting and find your passion. Go experiment and then let that guide your transition.

RESOURCES

The Alchemist by Paulo Coelho.

LESSON

Identifying your true opponent. Turn your focus inward and realize that YOU are your greatest opponent.

"PEOPLE WHO CAN CHALLENGE THEMSELVES
EVERY DAY HAVE THE BEST CHANCE TO IMPROVE
AND BE SUCCESSFUL."
NICK SABAN

RON "H2O" WATERMAN

IG: @ronwaterman | Twitter: @ronH2Oman | FB: Ron Waterman | ronwaterman.com

Former WWE and MMA star, Ron won the WEC Super Heavyweight Championship in 2003. Ron has fought all over the world, including five tours with New Japan Pro Wrestling. For more than a decade, he's been a featured speaker for the Team Impact motivational group. Today, Ron works as a Firefighter and Paramedic in Colorado.

ROUTINE

Give yourself some time to be alone. My devotional and workout time is a great way for me to get my mind right.

INSPIRATION

Our time in the spotlight may fade quickly, but we have a lifetime to impact others. Be a positive influence on your community.

MENTOR

Find that person you look up to who has a strong set of morals, character, and values. Take their advice and cherish it. Sometimes it's not their words, but their actions that are most impactful.

"PEOPLE DON'T CARE HOW MUCH
YOU KNOW UNTIL THEY KNOW
HOW MUCH YOU CARE."

THEODORE ROOSEVELT

PREPARATION

The work ethic I developed through athletics gave me the foundation I needed to achieve anything I put my mind to. I became a firefighter and paramedic in my 40's. It's never too late to find a new passion!

RESOURCES

Shaken and *This Is the Day* by Tim Tebow.

EXPERT TO NOVICE

Because of my learning difficulties, I developed a strong work ethic at a young age. I entered the UFC at 32 years old. I counted the hours preparing for my fights not in months or years, but decades. Determination and hard work go a long way. Obstacles are going to pop up, they are a test of how bad you want to succeed.

BILL NAGY

Professional Football

Risk Management Consultant, Financial Industry

ROUTINE

I feel like I have an advantage on the day when I workout in the morning. Everything else seems to fall into place.

MENTOR

There are many people willing to give great advice. Don't forget to give thanks.

> "A SHIP IN HARBOR IS SAFE, BUT THAT IS NOT WHAT SHIPS ARE BUILT FOR."
> JOHN A. SHEDD

CHALLENGE

I wanted to find success immediately. What I have found is that success is not a destination, but a journey. I have adopted the mentality of striving to improve each day. Success will come, trust the process.

LESSON

Focus on what's in front of you. Don't worry about things you cannot control.

MARC QUILLING

FB: Marc Quilling | LinkedIn: Marc Quilling

College Football

Sales Professional

LESSON

Never stop competing. Much like sports, business and sales are about competing, getting knocked down and getting back up.

GUIDANCE

Be open to trying new things. If you were interested in pursuing something in the past, but were limited due to academics, athletics, or life — why not start today?

EXPERT TO NOVICE

Like being a freshman, there is a bottom of the totem pole feeling. There is a lot to learn and others are much more knowledgeable than you. You need to be a sponge and take in as much as you can as quickly as you can to have a competitive edge.

"IF I HAD EIGHT HOURS TO CHOP DOWN A TREE, I'D SPEND SIX SHARPENING MY AXE."

ABRAHAM LINCOLN

DR. JIM TAYLOR

IG: @drjimtaylor | FB: Dr. Jim Taylor | LinkedIn: Dr. Jim Taylor

A formerly internationally ranked alpine ski racer, 2nd degree black belt in karate, and Ironman triathlete. Dr. Taylor is a Sport Psychologist who has worked with junior-elite, collegiate, Olympic and professional athletes over the course of three decades. He is the author of 17 books.

ROUTINE

Athletes who know what works for them and are well organized in their sport are the same ways after their sport ends. Athletes should apply the same practices that worked in their sport to other aspects of their lives, including school and work. Keys to a successful routine are knowing what needs to be done, doing what needs to be done, and holding yourself accountable for doing it well.

CHALLENGE

Both men and women struggle after sport with loss of identify and loss of social network. It depends on the individual. That's why it's so important for athletes to expand their self-identities and social networks before they leave their sport.

FORESIGHT

The most common mistake elite athletes make is not preparing for life after sport. Success after sport can't just begin when sport ends; rather, it must be planned for through education, financial planning, emotional preparation and expanding one's self-identity before retirement.

RESOURCES

My website drjimtaylor.com.

GUIDANCE

Get out of your comfort zone and expose yourself to new areas, including ones you might not think you'd be interested in. Think about the future now.

"GO BIG OR GO HOME."

JACKIE STILES

Twitter: @jackiestiles10 | FB: Jackie Stiles | jackiestilesbasketball.com

A basketball player at Southwest Missouri State and winner of the Broderick Cup for Collegiate Woman Athlete of the Year. Jackie was drafted 4th overall by the WNBA's Portland Fire in 2001, earning Rookie of the Year honors. She was inducted into the Women's Basketball Hall of Fame in 2016. Today, Jackie serves as an Assistant Women's Basketball Coach at her alma mater.

ROUTINE

Make sure you stay active. While playing a sport, you are used to the endorphin rush. When you stop cold turkey, it's easy to get depressed.

MENTOR

Be respectful of your mentor's time and be a great listener. Then when you are in the position to help someone, pay it forward. You can't accomplish anything great alone.

RESOURCES

Lead...for God's Sake by Todd Gongwer. This book had the single biggest impact on my post-athletic career. It helped me get my priorities in line.

I also find all of Jon Gordon's books very inspiring.

"IF YOU WANT TO BE GOOD, MAKE YOURSELF BETTER. IF YOU WANT TO BE GREAT, FOCUS ON NOT ONLY MAKING YOURSELF BETTER BUT THOSE AROUND YOU BETTER."

JIM HARSHAW JR.

IG: @jimharshawjr | Twitter: @jimharshaw | FB: Jim Harshaw | LinkedIn: Jim Harshaw Jr | jimharshawjr.com

Success Through Failure
PODCAST

All-American wrestler and three-time ACC champion at the University of Virginia. Jim represented Team USA in international competition. He served as the Head Wrestling Coach at Slippery Rock University from 2002-2004. His TEDx Talk: *Why I Teach My Children to Fail*, discusses failure as the path to success. Today, Jim works as a Motivational Speaker, Executive Coach, and hosts the *Success Through Failure* podcast.

FAILURE

I thought that because I was an elite athlete that I'd learned all the lessons I needed to know. I thought hard work would carry me through life. I was wrong.

Invest in yourself. Period.

Hire a coach. Get someone on your team who will continue to hold you accountable and help you see around your blinders. If you can't afford a coach, find a mastermind group.

LESSON

I learned that failure is a necessary step on the path to success. Failure is not an ending. It's a beginning.

GUIDANCE

Try new things. You don't have to commit to a career. Instead, have coffee with people who already do what you are considering. Shadow them. Read about them. Most passions are not discovered, they're created.

RESOURCES

Designing Your Life by Bill Burnett.

> "EVERYONE MUST CHOOSE ONE OF
> TWO PAINS IN LIFE; THE PAIN OF DISCIPLINE
> OR THE PAIN OF REGRET."
> JIM ROHN

FREDRIK EKLUND

IG: @fredrikeklund | Twitter: @fredx9

Professional Football
Regional Manager, Retail

INSPIRATION

You aren't 'football player Fredrik' — you are Fredrik who plays football.

> "YOU CAN, YOU SHOULD, AND IF YOU'RE BRAVE
> ENOUGH TO START, YOU WILL."
> STEPHEN KING

JASON FOX

IG: @jasonfox70 | Twitter: @jasonfox70 | FB: Jason Fox | LinkedIn: Jason Fox | earbudsmusic.com

Professional Football

CEO, EarBuds

PREPARATION

When I was playing for the Dolphins, an opportunity arose to work on my MBA during the off-season. I wanted to make sure I could have a smooth transition.

I decided to spend two off-seasons in a row to earn my MBA. It involved long hours and crammed schedules, but it was well worth it! The business education and connections have been crucial for my company's success.

EXPERT TO NOVICE

Take the mindset that you are going to learn every single day. The fear of failing or making mistakes was difficult to overcome. I've found the best way to deal with these challenges is to attack them head-on. Treat it like a marathon, not a sprint.

SPENCER BROWN

IG: @dartmouthstrong | Twitter: @dartmouthstrong | FB: Spencer Brown

College Football
Director of Strength & Conditioning, Dartmouth College

LESSON

Nothing is more rewarding than reaping the benefits of hard work. At the end of the day, you will see if what you did was enough. If not, adjust your approach and try again.

RESOURCES

Discipline Equals Freedom by Jocko Willink.

"IT ISN'T JUST WHAT YOU DO, IT'S HOW YOU DO IT."

LANCE BALL

IG: jerseyboi4life | Twitter: @lanceball35 | LinkedIn: Lance Ball

Professional Football
IT Sales, Zoom Video Communication

LESSON

Discipline is a big part of success.

"LET ME TELL YOU SOMETHING YOU ALREADY KNOW. THE WORLD AIN'T ALL SUNSHINE AND RAINBOWS. IT'S A VERY MEAN AND NASTY PLACE, AND I DON'T CARE HOW TOUGH YOU ARE, IT WILL BEAT YOU TO YOUR KNEES AND KEEP YOU THERE PERMANENTLY IF YOU LET IT. YOU, ME, OR NOBODY IS GONNA HIT AS HARD AS LIFE."

ROCKY BALBOA (ROCKY)

the Spaniard show

CHARLIE "THE SPANIARD" BRENNEMAN

IG: @charliespaniard | Twitter: @charliespaniard | FB: Charlie "The Spaniard" Brenneman | LinkedIn: Charlie Brenneman | charliespaniard.com

Charlie won the inaugural season of the TV show Pros vs Joes in 2006. By 2011, he was the seventh ranked UFC fighter in the world. A former high school Spanish Teacher, Charlie details his journey in his 2015 autobiography *Driven: My Unlikely Journey from Classroom to Cage.* Today, Charlie is a sought-after Motivational Speaker, and hosts *The Spaniard Show,* a podcast about learning.

CHALLENGE

It was the sacrifice, commitment, and hard work that gave me a sense of fulfillment. I redirected those traits in a new direction. I'm the same person just with a different purpose.

GUIDANCE

Commit yourself to being a lifelong learner.

"DON'T GO AROUND TELLING PEOPLE HOW GOOD YOU ARE, LET THEM TELL YOU."

BUTCH BRENNEMAN

RESOURCES

When you're a professional athlete, you're surrounded by world-class people every day. When you retire, all of a sudden, you're not.

I needed to re-create that environment in a consistent manner. I produce a daily podcast where I interview world-class individuals. You'll find all the information and resources I've gathered at (charliespaniard.com).

EXPERT TO NOVICE

You have world-class credibility in one area, but you haven't proven your worth in a new career. So what do you know? The truth is, you actually know A LOT. The challenge is striking a balance between listening to expert advice and following your gut.

MORGAN DENNIS MORRIS

IG: @morgandmorris | Twitter: @morgandmorris | FB: Morgan Dennis Morris

An eight-time All-American gymnast and NCAA National Champion at the University of Alabama. Morgan won New Jersey Optional Athlete of the Year in high school and competed at the US National Championships. She earned a Master's degree in Sports Management. Today, Morgan works as a College Athletics Administrator at The University of Cincinnati.

ROUTINE

Keep an exercise routine. As athletes, exercise is at the core of our identity. I took a break from working out after I was finished with gymnastics, partly because I knew I didn't HAVE to anymore. It was nice for a while, but then I had to get back on track. Exercise is a main source of my motivation, energy, and balance.

MENTOR

There are a number of ways to engage with influential people in different industries. Don't limit yourself to relationships only with other athletes.

I believe a great mentee listens, asks good questions, and also shows a lot of initiative.

PREPARATION

I utilized the resources offered by the athletic department, but I wish I took better advantage of the resources offered to the entire school. This would have allowed me to learn about myself as an individual outside of sports.

RESOURCES

Dr. Tim Elmore's Growing Leaders blog (growingleaders.com).

ALEX WUJCIAK

IG: @alexwujciak33 | Twitter: @awuj33 | FB: Alex Wujciak

A three-time All-ACC College football linebacker, Alex finished his career with nearly 400 tackles. In 2015, he graduated from the 155th New Jersey State Police Class. Today, Alex serves as a State Trooper in New Jersey.

INSPIRATION

No matter how long it takes, find something that inspires you to say, *I'm going to enjoy work today.* It doesn't matter how other people view it. At the end of the day all that matters is how you see yourself.

ROUTINE

Routine makes life easier. Make sure your habits reflect your goals.

LESSON

You will face obstacles and you will fail. Recognize obstacles for what they are and attack them head-on. Focus on making a difference.

> "NO PRICE IS TOO HIGH FOR THE PRIVILEGE OF OWNING YOURSELF."
> FRIEDRICH NIETZSCHE

NICOLE DEBOOM

IG: @nicoledeboom I FB: Nicole DeBoom I nicoledeboom.com

Professional Triathlete

Founder & CEO, Skirt Sports

SUPPORT

Celebrate other women! Sharing in others' success doesn't diminish your own. The more we encourage others as individuals, the more we all rise.

GUIDANCE

Here's the thing about passion. You can't force it. You can't decide to become passionate about something. But, you CAN tap into who you are today, right now and ask yourself:

When do I feel happiest and most alive?

Write down the instances when you feel like the best version of yourself. You will uncover common themes and something will become obvious. These are the things you should pursue.

The only thing you can control is yourself.

I've been copied, criticized, and sued. I've run out of money. I've hired the wrong people. I've made major mistakes with my product line, manufacturing, and marketing.

Through it all, I have never given up.

Obstacles exist to help us grow. There is always a solution to every problem, as long as you just keep moving forward.

Never, ever, ever give up.

MATT BIRK

Twitter: @birkmatt | LinkedIn: Matt Birk & Matt Birk and Company | mattbirkandcompany.com

A two-time All-Pro and six-time Pro Bowl selection, Matt won the Super Bowl as a member of the Baltimore Ravens in 2013. The Harvard University graduate played a remarkable 15 seasons in the NFL. In 2002, he established the HIKE Foundation, an organization focused on serving at-risk youth. Matt won the NFL's Walter Payton Man of the Year Award in 2011 for his commitment to improving childhood literacy. Today, he works as an Entrepreneur, Professional Speaker, and Author.

ROUTINE

It starts with clearly articulating your goal. This helps you define what is important and what isn't. If you are not intentional, your schedule can easily fill up with meetings and obligations that aren't helping you achieve your objectives.

Another thing is putting your phone away at night. Many people are always available, and therefore always working. Like when I played, leaving the facility meant I was done working. I find I am more effective; a better husband and father when I get away from work at night.

PREPARATION

When I was playing I didn't really make any preparations for life after football. Why? I think some of it was denial. I wanted to keep my focus on football so when it did end, I could say I was 100% committed.

I think this was a mistake.

I should have leveraged my platform as a professional athlete to network with business leaders and influencers. Those connections could have been valuable in helping me discern what I might be interested in pursuing when my career ended. Looking back, networking would have taken very little effort, and I don't think it would have taken away any of my focus from my playing career.

LESSON

Football taught me that I can do more than I think. It made me comfortable being uncomfortable. I have drawn on this when taking on new challenges. I don't know exactly how I am going to accomplish certain things, but I focus on the process and do the next thing well. As athletes, we know how to grind. That is an uncommon skill.

SARAH PARSONS WOLTER

IG: @spar27 | Twitter: @spars27 | FB: Sarah Wolter | LinkedIn: Sarah Wolter

Olympic Ice Hockey

Finance, Morgan Stanley

GROWTH

The running and spinning apps on my phone would be surprising to my 'former athlete-self.' I never exercised just for the heck of it — there was always a purpose. I would have laughed if someone told me while I was in college or training for hockey that I would start doing long-distance runs. But today, I'm so happy it's a part of my life.

"LIFE IS PRETTY SHORT. IF YOU DON'T STOP AND LOOK AROUND EVERY ONCE AND AWHILE, YOU MIGHT MISS IT."

FERRIS BUELLER

INSPIRATION

Remember the sacrifices you made as an athlete. Great successes don't just happen. You know what it takes to be great. Same process, different phase.

LESSON

Resiliency. In sports, the lows are incredibly low. But that's also what makes the highs so high. Having the resiliency to keep pushing forward has helped my professional career post-sports immensely.

MEDAL MIND

DR. JIM AFREMOW

Twitter: @goldmedalmind | FB: Jim Afremow | LinkedIn: Jim Afremow | goldmedalmind.net

An acclaimed Sports Psychologist, Mental Coach, and best-selling Author. In 2006, Dr. Afremow founded Good to Gold Medal, a coaching and consulting practice. He has worked with Olympic Teams & athletes from the USA, Greece, and India. Dr. Afremow assists athletes in the MLB, NBA, WNBA, PGA Tour, LPGA Tour, NHL, and NFL. From 2004-2013, he served as a Senior Professional Counselor at Arizona State University. Dr. Afremow's books include *The Champion's Mind*, *The Champion's Comeback*, and *The Young Champion's Mind*.

INSPIRATION

Peak performance is peak performance, so make life your new sport! Game on!

FORESIGHT

Some common mistakes that athletes make include: not keeping open communication with a support system to work through negative feelings and forgetting the importance of self-care. Mindfulness training and regular exercise reduce stress and keep us in a winning frame of mind.

"DON'T ONLY PRACTICE YOUR ART, BUT
FORCE YOUR WAY INTO ITS SECRETS,
FOR IT AND KNOWLEDGE CAN RAISE
MEN TO THE DIVINE."

LUDWIG VAN BEETHOVEN

It's important to realize that most athletes retire before age 40, then live a long time on memories.

Three tangible actions to better prepare yourself:

1. Experiment with new hobbies or interests.

2. Interview ex-athletes to hear their experiences and to get their recommendations.

3. Meet with a career counselor to explore possibilities.

GUIDANCE

Here are three useful self-reflection questions for discovering new passions:

1. How can I help others?

2. What gives me joy?

3. What gives me meaning?

JAMAAL JACKSON

IG: @Jamaal67 | Twitter: @Centerstage67

Professional Football
Radio Show Host

LESSON

Nothing lasts forever and at the end of the day, it's a business!

RESOURCES

The NFL Legends Community has a bunch of resources for just about any situation former NFL players may face (operations.nfl.com/the-players/nfl-legends-community).

NICK STEPHENS

IG: @nstephens3 | Twitter: @nstephens3 | FB: Nick Anthony Stephens | LinkedIn: Nick Stephens

Professional Football

Medical Device Sales

INSPIRATION

Knowing that progress is perfection helps you to become the best version of yourself. Trust your intuition.

"A SMOOTH SEA NEVER MADE A SKILLED SAILOR."
FRANKLIN DELANO ROOSEVELT

JAMILA WIDEMAN

Professional Basketball

Vice President of Player Development, NBA

INSPIRATION

You have a chance to be and to do anything you want – dream big!

"EACH OF US IS MORE THAN THE WORST THING WE'VE EVER DONE."
BRYAN STEVENSON

RUBEN GONZALEZ

IG: @thelugeman | Twitter: @thelugeman | FB: Ruben Gonzalez | LinkedIn: Ruben Gonzalez | thelugeman.com

An Olympic luger representing the Argentine National Team. Ruben is the first athlete to compete in four different Winter Olympic Games in four different decades (Calgary 1988, Albertville 1992, Salt Lake City 2002, Vancouver 2010). Ruben is a best-selling Author, his works include *The Courage to Succeed* and *Fight For Your Dream*. A Professional Keynote Speaker, he has worked with more than 100 companies on the Fortune 500 list. Currently, Ruben is training for the 2022 Olympic Games in Beijing.

LESSON

Resilience. After losses or injuries, you learn how to pick yourself up, dust yourself off, and get back in the game. Unfortunately, sometimes athletes sell themselves short. You have everything employers look for in an employee. The task is learning new skills and the willingness to start from ground zero.

ROUTINE

Every morning, I write down the most important 2-3 tasks I want to accomplish. That helps give my day a clear focus.

I also take a couple of 15 minute stretching breaks during the day. After

> ## "IF YOU'RE GOING THROUGH HELL, KEEP GOING."
> ### *WINSTON CHURCHILL*

each break I ask myself, "What can I do in the next 15 minutes to get me closer to my goal?"

PREPARATION

Do your homework. Google "a day in the life" of different jobs. Maybe you have an idea of what that role would be like and the reality is completely different. Search for people who do that job, call them up, ask to meet them for coffee and find out what it's really like.

RESOURCES

How to Win Friends and Influence People by Dale Carnegie.

Think and Grow Rich by Napoleon Hill.

The Magic of Thinking Big by David J. Schwartz.

Create Your Own Future by Brian Tracy.

Win Again!: Turn Athletic Excellence to Business Success by Mark Moyer.

GEAROID TOWEY

IG: @gagstowey | Twitter: @gearoidtowey | LinkedIn: Gearoid Towey |
crossingthelinesport.com

A rower representing Ireland, Gearoid competed in the 2000, 2004, and 2008 Summer Olympic Games. He is the Founder of Crossing the Line Sport, an organization dedicated to athlete mental health and transition out of sport.

GROWTH

Buddhify: meditation & mindfulness app designed for busy lifestyles.

Waking Up with Sam Harris: teaches meditation, how to reason more effectively, and deepens your understanding of yourself and others.

INSPIRATION

Don't isolate yourself. At first, it can feel like you're living on a completely different planet. Don't rush to be the king of a planet you know little about. Take time to figure out what stimulates you by observing and listening.

PREPARATION

You don't get the same level of feedback outside of sport. Being an athlete is black or white. Real life exists in the grey. You have to learn to live with that.

RESOURCES

Crossingthelinesport.com: an online community for former athletes focusing on life after competition.

OMARR SAVAGE

IG: @noturavgsavage | FB: Omarr Savage | LinkedIn: Omarr Savage

College Football

Registered Nurse

INSPIRATION

Meet new people with diverse backgrounds. Volunteering helped expose me to new ideas and forced me out of my comfort zone.

"IF YOU WANT WHAT YOU'VE NEVER HAD, YOU
MUST DO WHAT YOU'VE NEVER DONE."
THOMAS JEFFERSON

MENTOR

One tip for being a great mentee is to formalize some goals for the relationship. Sit down together and write it out. That way you're on the same page because you've clearly defined what you're working towards.

RESOURCES

Total Recall: My Unbelievably True Life Story by Arnold Schwarzenegger. I find Arnold is a perfect role model for people transitioning from one passion to the next.

LAUREN FITZPATRICK

IG: @lc_fitz

A lacrosse player, Lauren was Team Captain for the Lafayette Leopards in 2012. She is a three-time Patriot League Academic Honor Roll member and played in 62 games during her college career. Today, Lauren works as a Sales and Marketing Consultant for State Farm.

SUPPORT

Sometimes people think athletes are competitive machines who are too tough to show defeat. Not my group of friends. We share in each other's successes and in each other's hardships. The transparency of my support system helps me navigate those ups and downs.

GUIDANCE

Does anybody REALLY know what they want to do after college? Just keep saying yes to new experiences. Most importantly, be honest with yourself.

RESOURCES

The 12 Week Year by Brian Moran and Michael Lennington. This book helped me clearly articulate and refine my goals. It offers best practices for time management, how to define success, and how to manage expectations.

"WITH A LITTLE BIT OF DISCIPLINE YOU CAN DO A LITTLE. WITH A LOT OF DISCIPLINE YOU CAN DO A LOT. WITH TOTAL DISCIPLINE, YOU CAN DO ANYTHING."

LESSON

Learning how to manage personalities while working towards a shared goal is an amazing life lesson. You come across so many different types of people on an athletic field, and you don't get to pick who goes to battle with you.

EXPERT TO NOVICE

The greatest obstacle for me was getting comfortable feeling uncomfortable. Although athletics were mentally and physically challenging, I was comfortable.

When I began my career, I felt like I was completely reliant on other people for training. Having more questions than answers was unfamiliar and made me really uneasy, but that motivated me to learn all I could.

Slowly I've realized you can't learn it all in one day. An office runs very much like a team. My new teammates were very willing to help me get up to speed so we could excel together.

BRENT HAYDEN

IG: @thebrenthayden | Twitter: @thebrenthayden | FB: TheBrentHayden | LinkedIn: Brent Hayden | brenthayden.com

An Olympic swimmer, Brent won the 2007 Canadian Athlete of the Year Award and was inducted into the British Columbia Sports Hall Of Fame in 2013. He currently holds the Canadian record in the 50-meter, 100-meter, and 200-meter freestyle. Brent won the bronze medal at the 2012 Olympics in London, and gold at the World Aquatics Championships. Today, he works at Astra Athletica, an activewear clothing brand he co-founded, and exhibits his artwork in galleries in Canada and the United States.

CHALLENGE

After I retired, I was excited to begin the next stage of my life. Though I heard stories of athletes who struggled after sports, I thought I was emotionally prepared, and it wouldn't happen to me.

I was wrong. I quickly realized that without sport, I had no idea who I was anymore. I needed to rediscover myself, so I turned to fine art photography, a passion I had been pursuing during my swimming career. And then I began working on creating my business, Astra Athletica.

I think the best thing an athlete can do to prepare for the transition is to cultivate other passions while competing, so when the time comes, they're not dwelling on who they were as an athlete, but moving forward with who they will be.

> "SOME PEOPLE SHOOT FOR THE STARS, BUT PER-
> SONALLY, I DON'T LIKE TO SET LIMITS."
> *BRENT HAYDEN*

LESSON

The biggest lesson I learned from sports is to believe in your dreams because nobody else is going to believe in them for you. When I told people
that my dream was to swim in the Olympics one day, they laughed. They
told me it was impossible. They told me to get my head out of the clouds.
They told me I wasn't good enough. Not only did I go to the Olympics three
times, but I stood on the Olympic podium as a medalist!

MATT PHILLIPS

IG: @proathleteadvantage
| Twitter: @proathleteadvan
| FB: ProAthleteAdvantage |
LinkedIn: Matt-Phillips-Speaker |
proathleteadvantage.com

**A professional baseball player in Austria's Bundesliga and Division
I baseball player at Creighton University. In 2012, Matt founded Pro
Athlete Advantage, helping athletes and business leaders perform
their best. Today, he works as a Coach, Author, and hosts** *The Mental
Toughness Podcast.*

ROUTINE

When you start your morning in a productive and meaningful way, the rest of the day feeds off of that. I see too many ex-athletes stop working out all together, robbing them of the adrenaline boost and sense of accomplishment they were used to while playing. You have to keep familiar things...familiar!

MENTOR

Ask! Send an email or pick up the phone. Often they will say YES. Finding a mentor is not some contractual obligation, it's just two people getting together to have a chat. Really, just ask. It's truly that simple.

PREPARATION

Understand which skills have led to your athletic success. You understand the importance of preparation and how to handle adversity. Do those same things, just apply them to your new circumstances. You've done it before, so you can do it again!

LESSON

I control my destiny, no one else!

"IT'S NOT THE CRITIC WHO COUNTS: NOT THE MAN WHO POINTS OUT HOW THE STRONG MAN STUMBLES, OR WHERE THE DOER OF DEEDS COULD HAVE DONE THEM BETTER. THE CREDIT BELONGS TO THE MAN WHO IS ACTUALLY IN THE ARENA, WHOSE FACE IS MARRED BY DUST AND SWEAT AND BLOOD; WHO STRIVES VALIANTLY; WHO ERRS, WHO COMES SHORT AGAIN AND AGAIN, BECAUSE THERE IS NO EFFORT WITHOUT ERROR AND SHORTCOMING."

THEODORE ROOSEVELT

KIRSTEN BARNES

Olympic Rowing, Gold Medalist
Director of Performance Services, Canadian Sport Institute Pacific /
Mental Performance Consultant

INSPIRATION

Embrace the challenge of change. It takes time to step into a new phase of life. As my daughter reminded me when we moved, "Change is good."

GUIDANCE

Be curious! Give yourself a chance to explore different ideas and try things out. Even if you have to get a job solely for financial purposes, don't give up exploring. Everytime you try something, it gives you information for the next time.

"THE PATH OF LEAST RESISTANCE LEADS TO THE
GARBAGE HEAP OF DESPAIR."
MATT JOHNSON, SINGER

MACK FROST

IG: @frostee91 | Twitter: @frostee91 I FB: Mack Frost | LinkedIn: Mack Frost

College Football
Environmental Specialist

ROUTINE

I forced myself into the habit of waking up early. Take advantage of the time you have, otherwise the day can easily slip away from you. STOP WASTING TIME ON YOUR DREAMS.

Use social media, don't let social media use you.

"I AM GRATEFUL FOR THE LIFE GOD HAS
GIVEN ME. I AM FOCUSED, I AM DRIVEN. I
CAN DO ALL THINGS THROUGH CHRIST WHO
STRENGTHENS ME. I AM THE MASTER OF MY
FATE, I AM THE CAPTAIN OF MY SOUL."
MACK FROST AND W.E. HENLEY

MIKE ROBBINS

IG: @MikeDRobbins | Twitter:
@MikeDRobbins | FB: Mike Robbins |
LinkedIn: Mike Robbins |
mike-robbins.com

Mike played baseball at Stanford University, where he pitched in the
College World Series. He was selected in the 1995 MLB Draft by the Kansas City Royals, playing three seasons of professional baseball. Mike
has authored four books, including *Bring Your Whole Self to Work*. As
a Speaker, his clients include Google, Twitter, the NBA, and Microsoft.
Today, Mike works as an Author and hosts a weekly podcast.

It will be okay. You are not alone.

Allow yourself to feel sadness, anger, and fear, but also the excitement associated with starting anew.

CHALLENGE

My baseball career ended in the minor leagues when I hurt my pitching arm. I had four surgeries and wasn't able to come back. I dealt with physical pain, emotional pain, and feeling like I got a raw deal.

I feared I had blown my only shot to succeed in life. I felt alone. It was really difficult to process, so I reached out for support. With the help of a therapist, I dove deeply into personal growth for my own healing. This is what ultimately saved me.

"BE YOURSELF, EVERYONE ELSE IS ALREADY TAKEN."
OSCAR WILDE

RESOURCES

I love the TED.com website and app.

Books:

The 4-Hour Workweek by Tim Ferriss.

Way of the Peaceful Warrior by Dan Millman.

Don't Sweat The Small Stuff...and It's All Small Stuff by Richard Carlson.

Podcasts:

The School of Greatness by Lewis Howes.

Good Life Project by Jonathan Fields.

EXPERT TO NOVICE

One of the hardest parts of leaving sports and entering the "real world" is we as athletes don't like to suck at things. We're used to being good and winning. Life in the real world is humbling. At first, you are going to suck at the things you do, not because you don't have the talent, but because you're inexperienced. Focus on daily growth and try to enjoy that part of the journey.

TOM OTTAIANO

IG: @tomottaiano | Twitter: @tomottaiano60 | FB: Tommaso Ottaiano | LinkedIn: Tom Ottaiano | tbsmo.com

Professional Football

President & CEO, Today's Business / Managing Partner, Today's Athletes

PREPARATION

I searched to be part of a team again. I spoke to everyone I knew and reached out to the people I didn't yet know. Growing my network has led to my success in business.

RESOURCES

Shoe Dog by Phil Knight. Knight shares his path to success from an entrepreneurial standpoint.

Relentless: From Good to Great to Unstoppable by Tim Grover. Just as the title suggests, this book is all about being relentless in your pursuit of success.

"I DON'T WORK, I BUILD."

EXPERT TO NOVICE

One of my biggest obstacles was not fully understanding people's motivations. When you're an athlete on a team, there is an obvious common goal: everyone wants to win. On the business side of things, the lines are sometimes blurry. It can be challenging to unite everyone while still serving their individual wants and needs.

NINA RAGETTLI

IG: @ninaragettli | FB: Nina Ragettli
| LinkedIn: Nina Ragettli

Olympic Freestyle Skier

Fitness Coach

INSPIRATION

Be patient, you won't find a new passion overnight.

CHALLENGE

The loss of direct and immediate feedback was a challenge. Without a coach, I use self-reflection as a tool to get myself moving forward.

PREPARATION

I finished school even though I was traveling the world to compete. It was really stressful to maintain a schedule of school and skiing, but I'm really glad I completed my degree. You never know when or how your career will end.

"STARK SEIN BEDEUTET NICHT, NIE ZU
FALLEN. STARK SEIN BEDEUTET IMMER
WIEDER AUFZUSTEHEN."

(ENGLISH TRANSLATION)
"BEING STRONG DOESN'T MEAN NEVER
FALLING. BEING STRONG MEANS
ALWAYS GETTING UP AGAIN."

GARRICK CLIG

IG: @garrickclig | Twitter: @gclig | FB: Garrick Clig | LinkedIn: Garrick Clig

College Football

Trainer / Investor

GROWTH

Audible: this audiobook app has been a game changer for me because of my dyslexia.

Also, social media apps because of the anxiety associated with putting myself out there. Overcoming these fears of social media has been a breakthrough for me.

EXPERT TO NOVICE

One of the greatest obstacles for me in learning a new field was the belief that I was capable of learning something new. You can learn anything if you believe it!

ROUTINE

Dominate your morning routine. I begin my day by placing my hand over my heart, breathing through my diaphragm, and focusing on three things I'm grateful for. Being able to take a deep breath, having clients who want to work with me, and having a car. Keep it simple.

RESOURCES

Think and Grow Rich by Napoleon Hill.

The Success Principles by Jack Canfield.

The greatest lesson I learned from sports was that we're not that different from each other. We all have similar needs, fears, and desires. Great things are accomplished when we work towards common goals with other like-minded individuals.

> "SUCCESS IS THE PROGRESSIVE REALIZATION OF A WORTHY GOAL OR IDEAL."
> *EARL NIGHTINGALE*

WILL YEATMAN

IG: @willyeatman | LinkedIn: Will Yeatman

College Lacrosse & Professional Football
Commercial Real Estate Broker, Cushman & Wakefield

GROWTH

LinkedIn: I work on growing my network and utilize this app more than any other form of social media.

INSPIRATION

You're a competitor. Your next chapter should complement who you are as a person and what you've learned in the athletic arena. Don't let the mentality you've developed throughout your career go to waste!

CHALLENGE

I never wanted football to be my complete identity. That said, I really didn't have a clue what I would end up doing. I wanted to ensure the next phase of my life was nearly as competitive as the world of professional sports. Simply put, my industry is eat-what-you-kill. That brings out the best in people like me.

"DREAM AS IF YOU'LL LIVE FOREVER, LIVE AS IF YOU'LL DIE TODAY."
JAMES DEAN

RESOURCES

Shoe Dog by Phil Knight.

The New York Times and *Wall Street Journal*. I read the paper to understand what's happening around the world. I read the business sections daily and skim the rest.

If the newspaper is not your thing, subscribe to a publication like *The Skimm* that summarizes daily news so you can get up-to-speed on world events.

EXPERT TO NOVICE

I had to swallow my pride and let people know, oftentimes, that I was clueless. I'd spent over 10,000 hours watching film and mastering my craft in football, but I had no clue how to run a real estate transaction. Hell, I barely knew what square footage was! I took it upon myself to learn the national and international real estate markets like the back of my hand. It was the one thing I could control.

JOHN REGISTER

IG: @johnfregister & @silvermedal2k | Twitter: @jfregister | FB: John Register | LinkedIn: John Register | johnregister.com

A four-time All-American long jumper. John won a silver medal at the 2000 Paralympic Games in Sydney, setting the American long jump record in the process. He is a military veteran, serving in Operation Desert Shield and Operation Desert Storm. In 2003, John accepted a position with the United States Olympic Committee (USOC), and founded the USOC Paralympic Military Program which uses sports to assist in the recovery of wounded, ill, or injured service members. Today, John is the Founder of Inspired Communications, sharing his story of courage and inspiration through motivational speaking.

ROUTINE

Build habits into your routine that will last even after sports are done.

For example, if you are asked to go and visit with a sponsor, prepare as if you need a job now. This will shift your focus from showing up as the "celebrity athlete" to someone who genuinely wants to be in the room with a potential client who can hire you after your playing days have ended.

INSPIRATION

There is no linear path to success; it is paved with hard work, sacrifice, hills and valleys. Eventually, you will get there.

CHALLENGE

Loss of identity is real. Not being able to be on the field of play is like losing a limb. I know, I went through an amputation which temporarily ended my days as an athlete. It also ended a portion of my dreams. I was no longer going to be an Olympic hurdler. You can't run hurdles with one leg. And I was no longer going to be a military officer.

My advice is to know who you are outside of sports. You might not want to hear this now, but athletes get out of the game in one of three ways:

1. They win all the medals and age catches up with them.

2. A new crop of talent comes in and they can't compete.

3. They are shut down because of injuries.

My first retirement from Olympic sport came after an accident which resulted in the amputation of my left leg. My second retirement, this time from Paralympic sport, came because my body just could not endure the physical stress of working out.

Ensure you engage with your other interests regularly. This will make the transition easier.

RESOURCES

The Way We're Working Isn't Working by Tony Schwartz.

Leadership and Self-Deception by The Arbinger Institute. This book will change your life.

Think and Grow Rich by Napoleon Hill. This book will put you on a pathway towards purpose.

And, finally The Bible. The history lessons, psalms, and stories of overcoming adversity are encouraging when we feel inadequate.

LESSON

The greatest lesson I learned from sport is to make a path for the next generation. In spring 1983, Ken Handy wrote me a letter. He said, and I am paraphrasing, "Young Master Register, I am honored you broke my record in the long jump at Oak Park and River Forest High School. You have accomplished something very few others have done. I now pass on to you what was told to me when I set the record. All records are meant to be broken. Therefore, leave a legacy by being gracious to the person who breaks yours."

I have kept Mr. Handy's words in my heart of hearts. In fact, his words were the impetus of my decision to compete for the final time at the World Championship in Lille, France. I needed to finish in fourth place or higher in order to earn a spot for an American at the 2004 Paralympic Games in Athens, Greece. I finished fourth and secured a spot for a teammate. My lesson is always build a legacy.

"GO FORTH AND INSPIRE YOUR WORLD."

EXPERT TO NOVICE

My greatest obstacle was arrogance. I began a career after sports as a professional speaker. In my novice stupidity, I thought I was an 8 on a scale of 10. Then I went to the National Speakers Association annual meeting and realized I was a closer to a 3 on a scale of 15. If I wanted to be good, I would have to invest in being great!

You always, Always, ALWAYS have to get better at your craft. None of us have arrived.

JOIN THE CONVERSATION.

IF THIS BOOK HELPED YOU, TELL US HOW.

Share your story by reviewing The Transition Playbook
for ATHLETES on Amazon.

THANK YOU

TO EACH ATHLETE WHO GENEROUSLY SHARED THEIR TIME AND ADVICE.

COSTA

Thank you to my Mom, Dad, Sister, and Brother.

Thank you to Tony Lorine, an incredible mentor and friend. "Just don't stand like that."

Thank you to Nilay Sameer, your patience and determination is inspiring.

Thank you: Aaron Taylor, Alex Albright, Alex Wujciak, Barry Harper, Charles Sacco, Cooper Hospital Staff, Corliss Fingers, David Arkin, Dr. Jillian Ploof, Dr. Kelly Ryder, Dr. Mike Sasso, Edwin Williams, Gene Tosto, Greg Bradway, Greg Golden, Heather Arianna, Hudson Houck, James Dever, James Franklin, Jason Garrett, Jenn Cook, Jeremy Navarre, Jerry Jones & The Jones Family, Jerry McConnell, John Doherty, John Phillips, Kevin Kowalski, Kyle Jamaitis, Liz Motter, Montrae Holland, Nate Livings, Ralph Friedgen, Scott Swpoe, Sean Lee, Shaun O'Hara, Shawn Toner, Steve Saunders, Stephen McGee, The Bruvik Family, The Carter Family, The Curley Family, The Lafferty Family, The Stöckli Family, The Durkin Family, The Galt Family, Tim McDonald, Tom Brattan, Tom Dailey, Torrey Smith, Wade Phillips, and many more.

CURLEY

To Sarike, thank you for your unconditional love and support. Thank you Mom, Dad, Lauren, Kristin & Bob. Thank you Grandmom and the entire Lafferty family. Thank you to the entire Curley family. Thank you Marcel & Alice, Annemarie & Roger, Saskia & Phil, Maaike & Oli, Leonie. Thanks to all my aunt and uncles. Thanks to all of my cousins. Thank you to all of my coaches. And a special thank you to the thousands of teammates over the years who've been some of my greatest teachers and friends.

ADDITIONAL QUESTIONS

CHALLENGE

Athletes face a diverse set of challenges after sports. Studies show that men struggle the most with the loss of identity and women struggle the most with the loss of social network. Do you agree with the previous sentence and why? If not, please share your perspective.

FORESIGHT

What are the most common mistakes elite athletes make in their post-sport career?

GUIDANCE

You are asked to be a career mentor for recent student-athlete graduates. What advice can you offer about searching for and discovering a new passion?

INSPIRATION

Studies show about 50% of college and professional athletes struggle with the transition out of sports. In a single tweet, what encouragement or advice do you have for athletes currently struggling with the transition?

MENTOR

Everyone from coaches to teammates to family offer advice and act as mentors during challenging times. How did those people (or others) support you through your transition after sports? If YOU have acted as a mentor, please share your experience on the other side.

PREPARATION

While still playing, what are three tangible actions an athlete can take to prepare for "life after sports"?

RESOURCES

What resources would you recommend to athletes making the transition from sport? Why? (Books, websites, apps.)

CHALLENGE

Athletes face a diverse set of challenges after sports. Studies show that the loss of social network is the most frequently reported challenge women face after sports. What are other common obstacles female athletes can expect to encounter? Possible solutions?

ROUTINE

While playing, athletes' schedules are managed by coaches. What advice can you offer as the first step to creating a successful routine once sport ends? What are the keys to maintaining a successful routine?

SUPPORT

How can female athletes' best support each other, during and after the transition from sport?

RESOURCES

APPS

Acorn

Apple Books

Audible

Buddhify

Chakra Meditation

CNN

CogniFit

CorePower Yoga

CreditKarma

Fluenz

LinkedIn

Mint

New York Times

QuickBooks

TED Talks

theSkimm

Wall Street Journal

Waking Up with Sam Harris

BOOKS

45 - The Warrior Class by Alonzo Jones

Answer the Bell: Inventing Your Life as a Champion by Paul Vaden

Athlete's Guide to Career Planning by Petitpas, Champagne, Chartrand, Danish, and Murphy

Champion Minded by Allistair McCaw

Chop Wood, Carry Water by Joshua Medcalf

Confessions of an S.O.B. by Al Neuharth

Create Your Own Future by Brian Tracy

Designing Your Life by Bill Burnett

Discipline Equals Freedom by Jocko Willink

Don't Sweat The Small Stuff... and It's All Small Stuff by Richard Carlson

Drive by Daniel Pink

Eleven Rings by Phil Jackson

Extreme Ownership by Jocko Willink and Leif Babin

Fear is Fuel by Patrick Sweeney

Going to Pieces Without Falling Apart by Mark Epstein

Good to Great by Jim Collins

Grit by Angela Duckworth

How to Argue and Win Every Time by Gerry Spence

How to Win Friends and Influence People by Dale Carnegie

In Tune with the Infinite by Ralph Waldo Trine

Lead... for God's Sake by Todd Gongwer

Leadership and Self-Deception by The Arbinger Institute

Lean In: Women, Work, and the Will to Lead by Sheryl Sandberg

Man's Search for Meaning by Viktor Frankl

Outliers by Malcolm Gladwell

Post Moves by Angela Lewis

Relentless: From Good to Great to Unstoppable by Tim Grover

Shaken by Tim Tebow

Shoe Dog by Phil Knight
St*art With Why* by Simon Sinek
The 12 Week Year by Brian Moran and Michael Lennington
The 4-Hour Workweek by Tim Ferriss
The 7 Habits of Highly Effective People by Stephen Covey
The Alchemist by Paulo Coelho
The Ant and the Elephant by Vince Poscente
The Bible
The Magic of Thinking Big by David J. Schwartz
The Power of Moments by Chip and Dan Heath
The Power of Your Subconscious Mind by Joseph Murphy
The Story of My Experiments With Truth by Mohandas Gandhi
The Success Principles by Jack Canfield
The War of Art by Steven Pressfield
The Way We're Working Isn't Working by Tony Schwartz
Think and Grow Rich by Napoleon Hill
This Is the Day by Tim Tebow
Total Recall: My Unbelievably True Life Story by Arnold Schwarzenegger
Unlabel: Selling You Without Selling Out by Marc Ecko
Warfighting by U.S. Marine Corps Staff
Way of the Peaceful Warrior by Dan Millman
Win Again!: Turn Athletic Excellence to Business Success by Mark Moyer
You Are a Badass by Jen Sincero
Zen and the Art of Motorcycle Maintenance by Robert Pirsigr

PODCASTS

Good Life Project by Jonathan Fields
Master of Scale by Reid Hoffman
Sets For Life by Joi Walker
The Tim Ferriss Show by Tim Ferriss
The School of Greatness by Lewis Howes

VIDEOS
6 Rules for Success by Arnold Schwarzenegger

WEBSITES
athlife.com
athlifefoundation.org
charliespaniard.com
crossingthelinesport.com
drjimtaylor.com
growingleaders.com
linkedin.com/jonharris
myfitnesspal.com
operations.nfl.com/the-players/
nfl-legends-community
scholarballer.org
supportforsport.org
ted.com
wearegameplan.com

ATHLETE INDEX

CPSIA information can be obtained
at www.ICGtesting.com
Printed in the USA
LVHW080328200519
618431LV00010B/41/P

9 780578 457697